hamlyn | **all colour petcare**

games to play
with your dog

Contents

Introduction

Playing games comes naturally to dogs of all shapes, sizes and ages, and for puppies it's an important part of their physical and mental development.

No matter what breed or crossbreed you have – from the smallest miniature to the largest hound – you will find lots of ideas in this book to suit your pet. There are more than 70 games of differing complexity, from simple search-and-find games to garden activities that involve jumps, tunnels, hoops and paddling pools. You will find ideas for walks and games in the park; games designed to test your dog's mental agility; activities aimed at specific breeds; self-rewarding games for times when you need to leave your pup home alone; and ideas for energetic family fun that will entertain both humans and canines alike. There are even games designed to spice up your puppy's obedience-training sessions.

Many of the games are based on the fact that dogs love to hunt for food. You may not think that simply *searching* for a treat is a fun activity, but your dog would probably disagree. Dogs learn best when they are encouraged by your enthusiasm or given a combination of encouragement and food treats. Tell your dog the name of every game played, so that he comes to associate the sound of the name of the game with appropriate play behaviour.

Playing with dogs is all about having a good time, but all the activities in this book should be undertaken responsibly and safely. Some athletic breeds are easily encouraged into repetitive jumping and running, but this can cause muscle strain that leads to painful injuries. In particular, energetic games should not be played in very hot or humid weather because dogs can dehydrate quickly if too much play is encouraged in these conditions. The combination of energetic dogs and children can also be a cause for concern, so games that involve both should be supervised.

I am guessing that you bought this book because you love your dog and enjoy playing with him ('he' is used for consistency to refer to dogs throughout this book, but of course

all the games relate to female dogs too). I have thrown a great many tennis balls for my own Boxer dogs, even though they have usually come back in a state far too soggy for me to handle. It's great fun – all our family dogs have loved to play and I am smiling now as I write this, because I can still see them and hear their play-barking. I would be pleased to receive letters and emails from you telling me about your own favourite games and any unusual ideas that you have developed with your particular dog.

Dogs are our close companions and, like children, they learn to understand that play is different from the more serious side of life. I hope you enjoy this book as much as I have done the challenge of devising great new games to play with your dog. Have fun!

Treats and training

Bake your dog a cake!

All the games in this book are treat-based and the reason for
this is simple: dogs love treats. They will eat as many as they are
offered – large or small.

It's important that you monitor the amount
your dog eats during game sessions and
adjust his normal food intake accordingly.
Only at the early stage of introducing a new
game or aspect of training to your dog should
you give him encouraging food treats. In the

long term you can reduce the need for food
treats by using a clicker (see pages 10–11).

The right snacks

High-protein processed human foods, such
as cheese and chocolate, are not suitable
for dogs and can cause health issues. It is
important to avoid giving your dog *any*
human foods that contain additives such
as sugar and salt, as these can increase
hyperactivity in dogs.

Bought dog treats usually contain food
additives, although it is possible to buy
organic healthy treats. You can use a portion
of your dog's usual food as treats or even
make your own, like liver cake (see box).
Meaty treats are believed to be the best, but
I have known dogs to salivate over slices of
carrot or apple. It may be possible to offer
fruit or vegetables as healthy options, but
whether your dog enjoys them will depend
on his breed and individual temperament.

Liver cake

In a food processor, blitz 250 g (½ lb) freshly chopped liver, 500 g (1 lb) plain flour and 2 eggs. The mix should be like a soft, smooth pâté. If necessary add water, one tablespoon at a time. Spread the mixture evenly on a baking tray and bake in a preheated oven, 200°C (400°F), Gas Mark 6, for about 10–15 minutes. Remove from the oven when it is still slightly moist and not fully cooked. When the cake is cool, slice and freeze until needed. For an older dog, it may be appropriate to lower protein levels by reducing or removing the liver and egg content, replacing this with lightly steamed vegetables.

During the early days, keep plenty of treats ready in your pocket. After a few weeks your dog should begin to understand most of the basic instructions associated with each game. Dogs learn quickly if game sessions are enjoyable. Try not to become angry or disappointed if he initially fails to respond, for it can take a number of attempts to succeed in teaching a new instruction and frustration on your part will only confuse your dog. Reward with a click (see pages 10–11) and a food treat, together with praise or stroking, when he responds to a new instruction.

You should avoid exercising or playing with your dog when he is hungry, as this can lead to frustration and possibly aggression issues. Ideally, you should also let him calm down with a long-lasting chewy treat when the game has finished. If any games lead to frustration or over-excitement, choose calmer, slower-moving games instead.

Never punish

It is vital that you do not smack your dog or shout aggressively at him. Such actions will encourage mistrust and can even trigger aggression or nervousness in dogs. Shouting is effectively *barking* at a dog.

Clicketty-click
Speed up the learning process

A clicker is an optional but useful extra for the games in this book, except for the self-rewarding ones in which your dog has to reward himself, often while you are away from home.

Originally used on dolphins, clicker training is now accepted around the world as a superb method of training all animals, including dogs. It is based on a reward-based training known as 'positive reinforcement'. Once your dog has associated the clicker with tasty treats, you can use the double-click sound not only to speed-train him to understand games, but also to promote his best behaviour.

How clicker training works

The clicker works through the classical psychological-conditioning principle of 'association and effect'. The unique sound of the clicker becomes embedded in the dog's brain, especially when it has been associated with a special food treat. Eventually the sound of the clicker alone becomes the treat, and so the signal can be used – without treats – to reward your dog in the home and on walks. It should only take a few attempts and some tasty treats to condition your

puppy or dog to associate the sound of the clicker with food or 'reward'.

Introducing the clicker

With clicker in hand, but held behind you, instruct your dog to sit. The moment he responds, first sound the clicker and then follow this up with a food treat.

Walk away from your dog and, as he follows, instruct him to sit by your side again and repeat the click *immediately* when he responds correctly.

Click and play

You can use the clicker to help your dog learn a new game. First show him what you want him to do, then teach him to play following verbal commands alone.

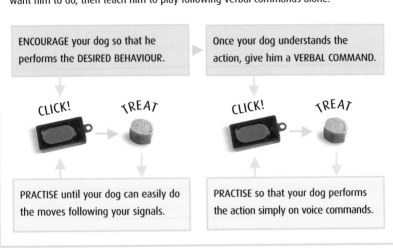

ENCOURAGE your dog so that he performs the DESIRED BEHAVIOUR.

Once your dog understands the action, give him a VERBAL COMMAND.

CLICK! → TREAT

CLICK! → TREAT

PRACTISE until your dog can easily do the moves following your signals.

PRACTISE so that your dog performs the action simply on voice commands.

Ask your dog to do a task (anything from giving a paw or rolling over to bringing a toy to you) and, as soon as he responds for the first time, click and treat him.

Next time, give him the same instruction and click (without offering a treat) as soon as he begins to respond, then click again (this time giving a treat) as soon as he has achieved the task. Then ask him to perform the same task, but use only the clicker.

During the first week it is advisable to use the clicker in the home or garden, where your dog's arousal levels are usually much lower than when he is out on an exciting walk. Once your dog fully recognizes the sound of the clicker as the reward, he will begin to respond to its use without too much encouragement. Initially the reward should be food-based, but eventually the reward (or 'reinforcer') following the sound of the clicker could be a pat or verbal congratulation such as 'GOOD DOG'. Continue the close association with food by clicking each time you offer your dog his daily meal.

Reward whistle

An exciting new sound

Like the clicker, a training whistle is another optional extra that can be used in the games. If it is introduced in a fun way, a whistle can encourage your dog's obedience and help him to respond more quickly to your commands.

A whistle can be particularly useful for recall on walks, as sensitive hearing will enable your dog to pick up its sound at distance and respond to your command. This will give you great long-distance control.

How the whistle works

Like the clicker, the whistle works by association, but this time to announce an instruction rather than just signal a reward. Put simply, the primary aim of the whistle is to gain your dog's undivided attention. Your dog will respond with an appropriate action, either to return to your side or to start a game. He can then be rewarded with a click, a fuss (on return) and a treat, depending on the situation.

Introducing the whistle

Initially introduce the whistle in random sessions a few times per day in your home, so that its use cannot be associated with other events or games that you are planning to introduce at a later stage.

Stand in a different room to your dog, or wait until he is in the back garden, and blow the whistle. In early sessions, calmly reward his obedience if he comes to you with a click, a food treat, a stroke and verbal praise. Later, you can give these rewards randomly.

Use the reward whistle every now and again around the home during the first few days and then expand its use to the back garden over subsequent days. Eventually use it for training exercises, on walks and in the games themselves. Use it proactively when introducing game sessions, during brief foraging games and when working with your dog on retrieval of a ball or Frisbee. Always use it for recall when he is off-lead on walks. Even if there is a delay in his return, offer him a click, a reward and a big fuss when he does come, to encourage future recalls.

training games

Musical commands
Who's top dog?

This game is like musical chairs, but with dog commands. See if
your dog can sit and lie down more quickly than your children!
This fun game for birthday parties helps to hone obedience skills.

What you need
- Children
- Chairs
- Music system
- Healthy treats
- Optional extras: training whistle, clicker

What to do

If your dog won't walk to heel, put him on
a short lead. Gather everyone in a circle
around a line of chairs, then take up your
position next to the music system to play the
'conductor'. It is your job to start and stop the
music and announce the command.

The conductor begins the music and, just
as in musical chairs, the children and dog
handler walk or run around in a circle. At a
random point the conductor stops the music

and says 'SIT'. At this, the children have to sit
on the chairs as quickly as possible, and the
handler gives the dog the command 'SIT' as
well. The last child down is out of the game.
The conductor then restarts the music and the
game continues, until one chair remains.

If your dog is struggling, you can give him
a head start by asking the handler to give the
command when the music stops, for both
children and dog to follow. The more dogs
that play, the better – but beware of creating
too much competition between proud dog
owners... this game could get catty!

Taking it further

You can vary the commands as your dog
becomes trained. Try 'DOWN' (children lie
down), 'BEG' (children kneel and then beg) or
combining commands: 'SIT' and then 'DOWN'.
A well-trained dog should stay in the
competition to the end. Praise or click for
every command that is successfully obeyed.

Recall relay
His master's voice

Teaching your dog instant response when you call him can be vital for walks off the lead. This is a simple game that will reinforce a fast response to the sound of his name.

What you need
- Family member or friend
- Optional extras: training whistle, clicker, stopwatch

What to do

Stand with your dog seated by your side. Your helper should walk a measured distance away (initially 30–50 strides). On your signal, the helper sounds the whistle (if he has one) and encourages your dog to come. When the dog is close to the helper, call him back by name in a clear, bright voice. As soon as he comes back, offer congratulations, together with a click (or praise) and a treat. You can turn this recall exercise into a game by using a stopwatch to time the speed of your dog's return over set distances.

Make the game more difficult for your dog by gradually increasing the distance between you and your helper. The helper can also try to distract your dog and test his obedience to your name call, by tempting him with a toy.

Competitive streak

If you really want to make a challenge out of this training, compete against your fellow owners, with the first dog to get to the helper and back declared the winner!

Give a paw
Say hello to your dog

When your dog has reached a certain level of training, it can be a smart idea to teach him a new trick. There are plenty to choose from, but this one is fun and simple for him to learn.

What you need

- Healthy treats
- Optional extras: training whistle, clicker

What to do

Teaching simple tricks to your dog is an effective way to exercise his concentration levels and stimulate his brain power. This one has the added bonus of impressing any visiting dignitaries!

Kneel in front of your dog and ask him to 'SIT'. Say 'RIGHT' and gently touch his right foreleg, then hold out a treat for him in your closed hand.

At this early stage, dogs will offer different reactions. If your dog nuzzles your hand or stands up, remain impassive. If he paws the hand containing the treat, congratulate him, click instantly to reward him and then give him a treat.

If your dog struggles to understand or is easily distracted, stare into his eyes while he is in a seated position and then use your hand almost like a paw, holding it out towards him. If you are lucky, he might mimic your action as he attempts to read your facial expression.

Once your dog has mastered the word 'RIGHT' and the associated action of raising that paw (the clicker will speed up this process), repeat the trick several times to reward each successful response.

The next stage of the game is to teach him 'LEFT' in the same way. Then start to teach him which paw to offer when you ask. If he raises the opposite paw from the one you have requested, gently knock it down, say 'NO' and touch his other paw. Many dogs will automatically lift the paw you have touched, in the hope of receiving more treats.

Socialization as a game
Getting to know the world

By far the most important aspect of puppy training is socialization. Games that get him accustomed to the vagaries of the world will help ensure he grows into a calm, confident, happy adult dog.

What you need

- Family and friends
- Pen and strips of paper
- Hat or container
- Props: Glasses, crash helmet, umbrella, bag, etc.
- Optional extras: training whistle, clicker

What to do

Involving children in socializing your puppy helps them understand the responsibilities of owning a dog, as well as giving them the chance to dress up, go to the park and interact in all sorts of different ways with their beloved pet.

First, sit down with your children and devise a list of things you want your dog to experience for the first time and with which he should happily associate. These should be scenarios the puppy will come across on walks, such as other dogs, busy streets and people with crash helmets, umbrellas or bags, as well as the potentially scary things he will encounter at home, such as vacuum cleaners, stereo equipment and other pets and children. Write the different scenarios and items down on strips of paper, then fold up the strips and put them all into a hat or some other container.

Every day invite a child to pick a piece of paper from the hat or container and read it out. The scenario picked is the one to act out. For instance, if 'glasses' is chosen, ask whoever chose it to greet your puppy wearing a pair of spectacles. If 'children' is chosen, allow the child to hold the lead as you walk your puppy in a playground (provided he has had all his vaccinations) – he is sure to get loads of attention from the children.

As with all socialization, ensure your puppy is happy and relaxed and monitor his mood constantly. Involving too many children in the process could be daunting for your puppy, so start with just one or two until your puppy becomes confident.

Playing for rewards

You can bring in a reward element for the children by listing the tasks on a chart and ticking them off as they are completed. When the family has finished ten scenarios, everyone is rewarded with a trip to the park, or a favourite activity from the 'Family games' section of this book (see pages 44–79). Another idea is to convert an advent calendar so each day contains a sweet and a scenario. Always check for signs of nervousness as the last thing you want is for your puppy to grow up frightened of children.

searching
games

Hidden treats

The game for busy owners

Searching out hidden food treats probably comes close to being the greatest pleasure your dog can experience. Quick and easy to set up, this is the game to choose if you don't have much spare time and want a surefire way of amusing your dog.

What you need

- Healthy treats
- Rice paper
- Dog gate or lead
- Optional extras: training whistle, clicker

What to do

This is one of the easiest search-and-find games to play with any dog breed. Any dog that doesn't enjoy tasty food treats needs to be seen by a veterinarian or pet shrink as soon as possible!

Wrap up to ten healthy treats in individual edible rice paper parcels, making larger parcels for a big breed and smaller ones for a medium or miniature dog. Wrapping them up can add a great deal of anticipation and excitement to the game when he finds them, although the hungry dog will probably 'wolf' them straight down, rice paper and all, without attempting to unwrap them.

Confine him behind a dog gate or secure him on the lead. Let your curious hound watch as you begin hiding each treat in different places.

Use easy hiding places for each treat at first, but once your dog knows the aim of the game and has played it a couple of times, start being inventive. Count out the treats so that you know how many he has to find. This is important when the game is being played in the home and he misses one – a few days and that lost treat will start to smell!

Search for novel places to secrete each treat: hide them in boxes and pots, or behind waste bins and garden ornaments. Bring into play ordinary obstacles in the house and garden that will help to conceal the treats

and task your dog's brain, tongue, paw and searching skills.

Now release your dog, blow the training whistle if you are using one, sit back and enjoy watching him frantically searching the areas where you have laid down those delicious treats. If you are using a clicker, sound it every time he succeeds in finding one. Some dogs will literally jump for joy when they locate a hidden treat, while others will quickly consume it and continue the search. What will your dog do?

Sherlock Bones
Follow that nose!

Your dog's nose is about 100,000 times more sensitive to smells than your own and following a treat trail will encourage him to use this incredible sense. Just watch him leap into action!

What you need
- Healthy treats
- Rice paper
- Dog gate or lead
- Optional extras: training whistle, clicker, stopwatch

What to do

Squeeze a handful of strong-smelling treats lightly between your palms and fingertips to transfer their distinctive and delicious doggy-treat aroma to you.

Put the treats to one side, then call your dog in a very happy tone and let him smell your hand. Announce 'TREAT TRAIL', before temporarily putting him on a lead or behind a dog gate. Offer him a single tasty treat in response to your 'SIT' instruction, but hold on to the rest of them, leaving him eager and wanting more.

Place the first of the treats on the floor a short distance away from where he is waiting. Make sure that he can see exactly where you are putting it.

Start laying a scent trail through your home and garden, stopping every few strides to rub a spot on the floor lightly with the hand in which you have held the smelly treats. Every five or ten strides put a treat down, sometimes choosing a spot close to a wall and at other times tucking the treat behind a chair leg or plant pot or some other obstacle. On the first occasion you should create a simple trail, but once your dog has got the hang of the game you can make the trails as complicated as his nose permits.

When you have laid out the trail, return to your dog, tell him to sit again and then let him off the lead or open the dog gate, at the same time saying brightly 'FIND'.

Click and count

If you have introduced a clicker (see pages 10–11), try clicking every time you put down a treat to let him know how many treats to expect. Even if he can't do the maths, you will work him into a frenzy of anticipation!

You can also click as he locates a treat on the trail, giving him a double reward each time.

Armed with a stopwatch, your family can also test your dog's trail speed at each session, challenging him to improve on his previous record.

Where's my parcel?

Is this for me?

Use an incredibly fresh or chewy treat and your dog's anticipation should go through the roof by the time you announce 'FIND'.

What you need

- Fresh, uncooked bone or large chew
- Large outer cabbage leaves or greaseproof paper
- Non-nylon string
- Dog gate or lead
- Optional extras: training whistle, clicker

What to do

This is an easy-to-perform game to be played in your garden or outdoor space.

Chop a large bone into 10-cm (4-inch) slices, reserving one and placing the rest in the freezer for another day (remove any marrow jelly, as this is too rich to be given in one session). Then wrap the bone slice (or a large chew) in the outer leaves of a cabbage or some greaseproof paper and tie it with non-nylon string into a loose parcel.

Show this to your dog in the home, saying 'PARCEL', or whichever word you choose to use. Then leave him, drooling, secured behind a dog gate or on a lead somewhere out of sight, while you proceed to hide the package in the garden.

For the first game, put it somewhere that your dog will find easily, so that he quickly learns what exciting event is about to occur. Say the word 'PARCEL' again and then say 'FIND', before releasing him to search. If he starts salivating, you know he is ready to play the food-parcel game.

Once he has learned what the game is all about, upturned plastic plant pots or empty cereal boxes are ideal hiding places to add a further challenge.

When he finds the parcel, he will have the further challenge of unwrapping it before he can eat the contents. Once the parcel string has been removed, take it away to prevent him accidentally swallowing it. If he licks the chew or bone for while and then leaves it,

use a plastic bag to pick it up and save it for another game.

If your dog seems at a loss while searching, go to the parcel and, after picking it up, wait a while before putting it down in a new place and announcing 'FIND'. His anticipation should now be at fever pitch. Some games just make you want to be the dog!

On the hunt

You can also play this game in one of your usual walk areas, but choose one where other dogs, which might also want to compete, are rarely encountered. First show the parcel to your dog, then hide it in a bag. Continue walking until your dog gives up pestering for it and, while he is off smelling scents, put down the parcel. Walk away from the spot and then, when you are at a reasonable distance from it, call him. When he comes, let him smell the hand that has handled the treat package, then say 'FIND' and watch him, nose down, start to use his superior skills to find his perfect reward.

Frozen food

Iced treats for dogs

In this outdoor game your dog has to wait for the thaw to occur, or lick like fury to obtain his frozen treat from inside a hollow toy.

What you need

- Semi-moist, tinned or dried dog food
- One or more foraging toys
- Optional extras: training whistle, clicker

What to do

This is a great variation on other games where concealment and freezing make for long-lasting fun (see pages 104 and 106). A standard hollow rubber foraging toy can be too simple for some clever dogs, which obtain the food from inside all too easily. By filling the toy with food and then freezing it, you can give your dog a bit of extra fun in trying to obtain his special treat.

Force-pack some of your dog's normal food into one or more of the toys. Place the toys in the freezer and leave them until they are rock-solid.

Call your dog in from the garden and leave him in a room where he can't see you hiding the frozen toys. Initially, you should conceal them behind obstacles where they can easily be discovered, but in later games you can make the search more difficult, perhaps by hiding the toys behind a rubbish bin or inside old packaging.

Sound the whistle, if you are using one, and set your dog off on his search. He may find the toys quickly, but it will take rather longer for him to get at those tasty morsels frozen inside.

Looking for leftovers
Is good food going to waste?

Instead of scraping food from your plate into your dog's dish, this game is about making him work for his dinner by hiding a trail of healthy leftovers for him to find.

What you need
- Healthy leftovers such as meat, fish and vegetables (avoid foods with sugar or salt additives and high-protein dairy products)
- Rice paper
- Dog gate or lead
- Optional extras: training whistle, clicker

What to do

Wild and feral (semi-wild) dogs are known to spend at least half their energy trailing scents in an endless search for food. These dogs live on their instincts when they are foraging in packs. You know your own dog better than anyone else. Will he follow scent trails as if he's part of a pack of hunting hounds, or will he simply sit back and wait for life to come to him? Instead of simply scraping leftover food into his dish, try playing this game to encourage your dog to work as hard as his wild ancestors. It's a golden opportunity to trigger his hunting skills and help him make use of his naturally enhanced senses.

If there are plenty of scraps left after your guests have gone home, choose appropriate non-processed foods, such as fat, meat offcuts, bacon rind, fish skin, chicken skin or vegetables. Chop these into bite-sized pieces and wrap them in edible rice paper. You can freeze some of the packages for use in subsequent games.

Secure your dog behind a dog gate or on a lead while you lay a parcel trail outdoors, then let him go. As he finds the hidden treats, sound the clicker or praise him to confirm his success. While this game is particularly suitable for scent-oriented breeds, any dog will thrill at a game that ends in a supply of the most delicious food scraps.

Lone wolf

You can also organize a trail in the part of the house or garden where your dog stays when you are out at work, college or any other activity that takes you away from home. He will discover the parcels after you have gone and may even congratulate himself on the successful use of his scent skills without any help at all from you, his usual source of food.

Treats by numbers

How many claps was that?

Goody bags containing treats will give your dog a really exciting reason to learn how to count.

What you need
- Healthy treats or small meaty chunks
- Rice paper
- Optional extras: training whistle, clicker

What to do

Lively herding breeds, such as Collies and German Shepherds, often excel at this game, although it can be mastered by most dogs. A canine genius may learn to look for many treats, but you should only play with as many treats as you think it is healthy for him to consume in any one game.

Wrap a number of healthy treats or small meaty chunks in individual rice paper wraps. Start by teaching your dog a simple association. Clap or sound a training whistle, then throw a treat in the opposite direction to him. Watch him race after it. Repeat this several times in a day, leaving a period of 10–20 minutes between each throw.

At the next stage, clap or whistle twice, then throw *two* goody bags in different directions. Repeat this stage on the same day, leaving some time between sessions.

If your dog looks for further treats after he has already located the two goody bags, say 'GAME OVER' and do not offer him any other attention. He should soon learn that these words mean the session is complete. It is not the meaning of the words, but the sound of them linked to the end of the session that he will come to understand.

Play the two-claps, two-treats game for a couple of days, before going on to the next stage in which you clap or whistle three times before tossing the appropriate number of goody bags in three different directions. With a little patience, this game can easily become a Greyhound-type race for your dog, in which he burns up any spare energy while you sit and relax.

Hidden toy

Where's it gone now?

This search-and-find game is ideal for a cold, wet and windy day when the great outdoors looks far less inviting than normal.

What you need

- Dog gate or lead
- A favourite toy or a special new one
- A discarded item of clothing that you have scented by wearing or sleeping in overnight
- Healthy treats
- Optional extras: training whistle, clicker, stopwatch

What to do

Put your dog behind a dog gate or on a lead, so he can watch what you are doing and learn that this is an exciting searching game.

Use a new toy, or a favourite one that is not used for retrieval (such as a ball or Frisbee) and that has not been played with for some time. A tug-of-war or rag-rope toy is ideal. Show this to your lethargic dog and watch him suddenly spring to life and become eager to play.

Wrap the toy in the item of clothing that you have scented. Leave a treat in a number of places to keep up his search interest, then finally choose a location for the toy, such as under the corner of a carpet, behind a box or below a table.

When you are ready, send your dog out to 'FIND' and praise him, even if he searches in all the wrong places. If he finds a treat, sound the clicker or praise him to signal that he is getting warm.

When he finally locates the toy, your scent around the old clothing will make the find extremely exciting. If you have a training whistle, sound it as he unravels the bundle to signal retrieval. When he returns to you with the toy, let him play with it for a while and then exchange it for a big hug and a few treats. Always put the toy away in a safe place after the game has finished so that its novelty is maintained.

Dinner work

Where's my meal gone?

This game is about making your dog work for his dinner, using his natural hunting and foraging skills to search out his daily food allowance. Eventually, the game can become as complicated as his instincts permit.

What you need

- Dog gate or lead
- Your dog's daily food allowance
- Three or more dishes (paper party plates are ideal)
- Healthy treats
- Optional extras: training whistle, clicker

What to do

Instead of simply offering your dog his food in a dish ('How boring is that', I hear him bark), organize a fun-filled foraging game using his normal food allowance.

Few non-working dogs have to perform a task in order to be fed. This can mean that clever working breeds develop a kind of food disinterest or boredom. It is common to offer a dog his daily food allowance in his dish. More often than not, he will either polish off the lot or leave a bit. In these situations the food dish is then refilled or cleaned and put away until the next meal time. Many dogs will just graze as the mood takes them, and any potential for mental stimulus related to feeding is lost. Look at your dog and notice his bright eyes when you change your way of offering him food.

First, contain your dog in the home, ideally within sight of your outdoor space, behind a dog gate or glass door or on a lead.

Place measured amounts of his daily food allowance in three dishes. Cover or hide the food, perhaps inside old packaging or under disused boxes or upside-down plastic plant pots. In poor weather you can use an easy-to-clean area of the house. Use at least half (if not all) of your dog's normal food ration. The first time you play the game, make one

of the portions easy to locate, with the others less accessible.

Release your dog to seek and locate the hidden food. Instruct him to 'FIND' the food. When he does, say 'YES' brightly, or use your clicker.

If your dog initially searches in the wrong places, sound a training whistle (if you are using one) and redirect his search by pointing the way for him. Be ready to congratulate him verbally or click when he locates any of the target food. As he progresses, try laying the trail when he's not watching. The number of food portions and difficulty of locating them can be increased, to challenge even the most intelligent of dogs.

Memory munch
Mmm, where did they go?

Can your dog really remember where you put each of those great-smelling treats? Test his brain power and create a great game for all hungry dogs.

What you need

- Healthy treats
- Rice paper
- Dog gate or lead
- Optional extras: training whistle, clicker, stopwatch

What to do

Plan out a memory game based on hidden treats. It is advisable to start the first game with a low number of treats and then increase them, not exceeding a healthy number of treats in one session. Wrap up to ten healthy treats in individual rice packets: large ones for a big breed; small ones for a medium or miniature dog.

With your dog behind a dog gate or on a lead, let him watch as you hide each treat. To emphasize that one is being placed, particularly when playing this game for the first time, you can sound the clicker.

If the game is being played indoors, now take him outside – or vice versa. Walk him back to the place where the treats have been hidden and say 'MEMORY MUNCH', then release him. See if he can locate all the treats. If you are using a stopwatch, see how fast he can complete the task.

As your dog searches, be ready to click as soon as he moves close to a treat. If he locates every one, he becomes a champion memory dog. If he searches in the wrong places, make the game even easier by leaving out the treats rather than hiding them.

family
games

Which hand?

Trick-or-treat for dogs

There are times when you may be too busy to play anything complex.
Here's a simple guessing game that all family members can play.

What you need
- Healthy treats
- Optional extras: training whistle, clicker

What to do

This instinct game challenges your dog to solve a simple food-detection task and will be enjoyed by all members of the family, from the oldest to the youngest. A fun way of offering food treats, it is also an excellent means of rewarding your dog after he has undertaken a task. Try playing it after he has had his muddy paws cleaned or has gone outside to relieve himself. He will quickly learn that if he performs a particular task, or is calm and patient while something is done, this game will follow.

Instruct your dog to sit. Then take a treat and place it on your open palm. Pass it between both open hands, in a slow and deliberate way, so that he can watch what is happening. Close your hands, then place them behind your back, before bringing one hand in front of him.

Ask in a bright voice 'THIS?' Then replace it with the other hand and say 'OR THIS?' With both closed fists outstretched, say brightly 'WHICH HAND?'

Let your dog sniff or lick your hands initially, especially during early attempts at this game. When he shows a preference for the fist that has the treat inside (some dogs even learn to paw the correct fist gently), say 'YES' in a congratulatory way. If he goes to the fist *without* the treat, say 'NO' in a sad tone, then show him both open hands so that he learns by his mistake.

Your dog will soon learn that the fist with the treat smells stronger than the one that is empty. Some dogs give a friendly woof when they think they know the correct hand. With small dogs, it is best to play when you are seated.

Going undercover
Into the underworld

If your dog enjoys burrowing – even if it's only underneath the sofa, table or duvet – this game is one for him and the children to play. In fact, it's the one they've been waiting for all day!

What you need

- Children
- Old duvets or sheets loosely tied or sewn together to make one big cover
- Healthy treats
- Optional extras: training whistle, clicker

What to do

Young children like nothing better than playing under sheets, creating tents or dens. In this game you will need to spread a giant cover over the floor or, if it's a dry day, outside on the grass. The bigger the cover you use, or the more sheets you can sew together, the better.

Put your dog temporarily in another room until the game is ready for him. Give each of the children a handful of treats and tell them to crawl under the cover. Then give your dog a pat and a treat, and send him to find the children who have hidden themselves under the cover.

Your dog will probably approach the cover with a mixture of curiosity and trepidation. Once he learns the game, he will know that the aim is to go under the cover to find out where the children are. Tell them to be playful and to roll about (but your dog might jump on the cover, so be wary of this if he's a hefty giant).

The children shouldn't give the dog any treats unless he comes under the cover. If necessary, lift up a corner of the cover and encourage him to crawl under it. If he

needs extra encouragement, ask one of the children to hold out a treat-clenched fist just within sight, to let him know they have the treats waiting for him 'undercover'.

The children should do their best to keep hidden, and can crawl or roll away from him. However, as soon as his wet nose has located them, they should offer him a treat as a reward.

Children find crawling under sheets particularly thrilling, so this could be the game to play when the nephews and nieces are bored and want to play with doggy – but make sure that neither children nor dogs overdo the excitement!

Magician's cups
Which of the three?

A little bit of magic might already exist between you and your dog, but in this game you or your children can play magician to his role as the attractive assistant.

What you need
- Healthy treats
- Three opaque plastic cups
- A table
- Optional extras: training whistle, clicker, someone to watch the show

What to do

This is another rainy-day game that can be played with all but the most hyperactive dog breeds. It offers a new way of encouraging your dog to use his nose.

With a handful of treats and the three cups at your disposal, metaphorically draw the stage curtains, instruct your dog to sit next to the table and prepare to do magic. Offer your dog a treat or two to keep his attention as he waits in the sit position.

Place the three cups, inside each other, on a table. Then line them up, facing the right way up, and pop a treat into one. Rattle the treat around the cup – especially for those dogs that like a sound-cue.

Turn all the cups over, facing down. Lift up the cup with the treat, nudge the treat so that your dog can see and smell the reward, and then demonstratively place the cup back over the treat.

On the first round, stir that cup – the one with the treat beneath it – around between the other two, making sure that it finally ends up being the cup closest to your dog.

Say 'WHERE?'— and hope that he sniffs the obvious. If his nose goes to or touches the right cup, offer lots of praise, lift the cup up and say 'OK'. As he takes the treat, continue your praise.

If, at this early stage, a hungry dog just gives you a dumb stare, encourage him by wobbling the treat cup. If he sniffs the wrong

cup at any stage, say 'NO' in a sad tone. On the other hand, if your dog can follow the table trick like an old professional, be ready to use swift hand movements to enhance the illusion. Children should be ready to do the audience applause once he has figured it out and spots the cupped treat with every move you make.

Bingo
It's all in the cards

Playing bingo with family, friends *and* your dog puts a fun twist on a favourite party game.

What you need
- Family and friends
- Large paper squares, numbered 1–50
- Old pot or bowl from which the numbered squares can be drawn
- Bingo cards, or blank postcards marked up with ten blank squares
- Healthy treats
- Optional extras: training whistle, clicker

What to do

If you are making your own bingo cards, shuffle all the numbered paper squares and place them in the pot, then ask family or friends who are playing to draw out ten papers each at random. Players then write their chosen numbers on to the blank squares drawn on their postcard. Alternatively, give each player a pre-printed bingo card.

Now fold up the numbered paper squares, with a single treat in each one. Return all the folded papers to the pot. Call your dog and offer him the bowl of paper packages. As he pulls one out, ask him to 'GIVE'. Unfold the paper square and, after instructing him to sit, give him the treat inside and offer him lots of praise. Announce the number on the square to everyone who is playing and mark off the number if it appears on your card.

The person to your right then offers the bowl to your dog so that he can select another square, and this continues until someone shouts 'HOUSE' when all their card numbers have been marked off.

If your dog is the kind of companion animal that wants to wolf the treat straight down – paper and all – it might be advisable to make the numbered squares out of tough cardboard. Be careful not to let him choke on the wrappings, and adjust his regular food intake according to the number of treats that he eats during the game.

Hide and seek
Coming, ready or not!

This is one of the easiest games to play as a family and helps teach your dog to search for an individual person.

What you need
- Children
- Healthy treats
- Two training whistles
- Optional extra: clicker

What to do

Your dog will already know all the individuals in your immediate family by smell and by sight. This game will help him get to know each individual by the sound of his or her name as well.

The hider should offer your dog a treat, but before giving it, should announce her name clearly, for example: 'SALLY'. She should repeat the name several times and, if using the clicker, sound it before saying the name again and giving the treat.

Your dog needs to wait for the 'FIND' instruction. If he won't sit until you tell him to move, hold him on the lead. Send the hider off with a whistle to hide (somewhere obvious in the first round). Once hidden, the hider can blow the whistle. This gives extra directional information to help dogs that are not brilliant at scenting and searching.

Say to your dog 'FIND SALLY' and blow your whistle, then encourage him to head in the right direction.

When the hider has been discovered, she should blow the whistle again and offer your dog a treat or two and a big fuss or cuddle. The hider can also say her name out loud again, to enhance this part of the learning.

Once your dog has played the game with several family members, the sound of each name should become associated with its owner in his memory. Then you can impress your friends by sending your very clever canine off to find a particular individual.

Singing class
Name that tune

Just how harmonious this musical game will be depends on whether you and your dog agree on a preference for heavy rock or acoustic ballads.

What you need
- Healthy treats
- Children
- Music system
- A couple of favourite tunes or recorded TV soundtracks
- Optional extras: training whistle, clicker

What to do

Before undertaking this game, it is important to consider that teaching dogs to bark can potentially result in antisocial behaviour. However, if your dog is not a natural barker, he can be taught carefully to use his 'voice'.

Dogs have a higher and more sensitive hearing range than humans and, as a result, can be encouraged to 'sing' when they detect a particular tone. The secret behind this game is understanding that dogs are a sub-species of wolf and not only use a low-tone play-growl to challenge one another, but the same wolf-like high-pitched howl to call out to each other.

When singing class is about to start, call your dog and offer him a treat or two to give him the idea that something good is going to happen. Start by trying to howl yourself (or getting the younger members of your family to do so), without any musical support. Imagine that the full moon is up and do your best werewolf impression.

Some dogs will immediately join in – this is the time to praise and use a clicker if you have one. Like people, dogs may sing sweetly, out of key or not at all. Some dogs will offer a mystified look and then disappear to hunt for anyone who hasn't gone to the dark side. If your dog joins in, go to the next stage.

Choose a musical track for your singing class that has distinctively low and high

pitches. If your dog already shows a vocal interest in a particular song or the soundtrack of a favourite TV show, you could record the music for playback. Play your chosen recording and, when the higher pitch comes in, start singing and take the pitch even higher so that it is close to a howl. If your

dog joins in, everyone can sing together like a pack of musical mutts.

This is when your singalong really starts to be fun. If your dog is called Prince, then your musical class should sound almost funky! Lots of praise and treats should be introduced as and when your dog is ready to take a bow.

Chew chase

Hot on your heels

Does your dog love to chase anything that moves? This game is perfect for chasing dogs – and it will tire everyone else out, too!

What you need

- A tough meaty chew
- Soft rope, 3–5 metres (10–16 feet) long, depending on age of human players
- Older children or energetic adults
- Optional extras: training whistle, clicker

What to do

If your dog is the type to run after anything that moves, this sometimes troublesome behaviour can be redirected into a great game. As usual, tell your dog the name of the game before starting to play so that he associates the sound of the name with appropriate play behaviour.

Tie the meaty chew firmly to the end of the rope, then put your dog on the lead and prepare whoever is going to drag the roped chew. If you have a whistle blow it, then say in a bright voice 'CHEW CHASE'. As you release the dog, the person on the rope should throw the chew as far as he can.

As the dog runs towards the roped chew, the person on the other end of the rope can pull it back and throw it again, before taking off on a run around the garden or park. Eventually the dog will grab the chew, or the rope if he's smart. When he does, praise him and let him feast on his reward.

Greyhounds, Whippets and Lurchers will love this game, although you'll have to be quick! It is best to play the game over short periods only so that the dog does not become over-excited, and always make sure that he is allowed to enjoy his prize as soon as he has got hold of the chew. Don't tease a dog that is trying hard but not succeeding, as this could lead to frustration and even encourage hyperactivity. Younger children may not know when to stop, so play the game with older children. Common sense should prevail at all times.

Fishing for dogs
A treat on the line

This is a great way for children to play chase without getting their hands near your dog's jaws. Whatever style of fishing rod is used, make sure your dog isn't left muttering about 'the one that got away'.

What you need

- Children
- Length of strong string or soft rope
- Strong garden cane or smooth pole
- Tough treats or toys
- Optional extras: training whistle, clicker, fishing reel

What to do

Make your rod by attaching a length of string or soft rope to a garden cane or pole, adding an old fishing reel if you have one (alternatively, for miniature breeds you could buy a child's fishing rod). Fix a decent-sized treat or toy firmly to the end of the line.

Call your dog and get him ready in a sitting position in the garden, wondering what is going on – just like a Greyhound waiting in the traps at a dog race. The player should say 'FISH' and flex her fishing rod, before sending the roped treat or toy flying. If your dog is not already out of the traps, send him off to chase after it. If he bounds up and almost grabs the reward, the player can flick the rod away again.

When he finally traps the treat or toy, the player should click or praise the dog and release his prize (if he hasn't already chewed it off) and let him eat the treat or play briefly with the toy. Then she can call him back, rebait the line and repeat the fishing expedition. After a fine catch, everyone can retire to the cooler and grab a drink. Fishing can be so exhausting!

Find the clues
Play detective with your dog

In this family-fun game, your dog's brain and nose combine to track down a missing box that is hidden in your home.

What you need

- Children
- Set of numbered clue-cards
- Healthy treats
- Small cardboard box
- A special chew (for the dog) and a chocolate bar (for the children), to be placed inside the box
- Optional extras: training whistle, clicker, stopwatch, spyglass, detective's hat

What to do

Nominate one of the children to create a set of clues written on postcard-sized pieces of card. Invite another eager volunteer to play the detective. The first clue-card should state where the second clue-card – and a dog treat – can be found. So it might read: *'If you go into the kitchen, look for something that receives a signal and you may get lucky!'* This indicates that the next clue-card (with its dog treat) lies near the kitchen radio. In turn, this clue-card might suggest that the bathroom holds the next clue-card (complete with doggy reward), and so on. The final card indicates the location of a secret box containing the prizes: a chew for your clever dog and a chocolate bar for Sherlock.

Once the clue-setter has hidden all the cards, treats and the box, the detective and his faithful hound can be summoned and given the start card. They then enter the first room and work together to locate the clue-card and dog treat.

Use a stopwatch if a little tension helps to make the game more exciting, giving the adventure a reasonable time limit. If the detective and dog find all the clue-cards, treats and hidden box within the allocated time, they have solved the mystery! Hounds, Pointers and Spaniels instinctively find this game very exciting.

Pet points

You can also use a points system. If the dog locates the treat (and thus the card) while Sherlock is still puzzling, five points are given. If the card is in a position where the dog cannot reach it, but he still indicates where the card and treat are (click or praise and give him the treat), then ten bonus points should be awarded. Otherwise, give a single point for each find.

Help me!
A game of lost and found

Within your companion animal there may lurk a mountain-rescue or earthquake-sniffer hero. This game checks out his credentials and reveals if it's worth loaning him to the fire service!

What you need

- Children
- A pile of clean rubbish, such as cardboard boxes and old clothes
- Dog gate or lead
- Healthy treats and a meaty chew
- Optional extras: training whistle, clicker, stopwatch

What to do

One player sneaks off to play the part of the desperately trapped victim. She might decide to lie down in the garden or upstairs in a bedroom, but wherever she chooses to hide a member of the rescue team throws old clothes or a pile of clean rubbish on top of her. Keep your dog behind a dog gate or on a lead until the game is ready to commence.

When the trapped one is ready, give your rescue dog a pat and a treat, and prepare to send him on his way.

The trapped one should begin moaning 'Help me, I'm trapped', in the best play-panic voice possible. It is helpful if the yells are high-pitched, because dogs recognize these sounds as submissive and as a plea for help or investigation. If you are using a training whistle blow it, then release your own version of Lassie and watch him go. He may realize that it's only a game, or he may believe that a member of his human-canine pack is in urgent need of his assistance.

Follow your dog, giving him plenty of encouragement on the way, especially if he's going in the right direction. Sound the clicker or use praise to reward his success. The trapped one should reduce the volume of her cries so that they fall to a whisper, and eventually go completely silent. Now your dog has to find her before it's too late.

When your dog has located the place where the victim is about to expire, give him lots of encouragement to pull off the rubbish or old clothes. If he looks a bit clueless, tell the trapped one to give out a long moan and to kick out a leg – that should do the trick. When your dog hero has finally found and freed the victim, he should be fussed over, patted and given a meaty chew as a reward. You can also challenge your dog to find the victim against the clock, using the stopwatch.

Find the bomb
Time is ticking away!

Is there a hero hiding underneath your dog's furry coat? This is a game in which he imagines he can save the lives of the whole family in a race against time.

What you need
- Children
- Egg timer/mobile phone
- Strong-smelling, meaty chew
- Cardboard box or strong parcel paper
- Dog gate or lead
- Optional extras: training whistle, clicker, string

What to do

Nominate at least one child as the searcher, and another as the bomb hider. Give the child who is doing the hiding an egg timer, which should be set to go off, bomb-like, in ten minutes or more (alternatively, use the alarm on a mobile phone). Place the timer alongside a meaty chew in a medium-sized box, or wrap up both in parcel paper. If your dog is the Hound of the Baskervilles type, it may be useful to loosely tie up the box or parcel with string.

Ask the searcher to show the box or parcel to your dog, gently placing it close to one of his ears so that he can hear the ticking and then restrain him behind a dog gate or on the lead. The child who is doing the hiding can then take the 'bomb' and put it in a secret place.

In the first game, as your dog is learning, the box or parcel should not be too difficult to locate. Later, when he has understood what is required of him, the children can make the location more difficult to find.

When the searcher and the newest recruit to your bomb-disposal team are ready, release the dog (if you have a whistle, blow it to signal the start). The searcher should instruct the dog to 'FIND THE BOMB', putting lots of emphasis on 'BOMB' to help him associate the word with this particular game.

If your dog starts looking in the wrong places, tell the searcher to draw him away in the correct direction with the training whistle. Repeat 'FIND THE BOMB' and sound the clicker or praise him as soon as he is searching in the right place.

Once your dog closes in on the pretend bomb, begin to encourage him verbally. When he finally discovers its whereabouts, let him have the box or parcel and see how long he takes to open it up – he may need help at this stage. (If you have used string, take it away once it has been removed to prevent him accidentally swallowing it.) Try to stop the alarm from going off as the doggy hero tucks into his meaty chew. Once the game has been successful, everyone should retire for a celebratory snack. Since you have been saved, proceed to sigh with relief and enjoy the rest of the day.

Where's that stash?

The reward money is waiting

There is a big fat reward for whoever can find the proceeds from a local robbery. Will your dog be the one to lead you to the cash?

What you need

- Children
- Sweets or small toys for the children
- Strong-smelling, meaty chew
- Cardboard box or strong parcel paper
- Cut-up newspapers representing wads of banknotes
- Dog gate or lead
- Optional extras: training whistle, clicker, string

What to do

This is a variation on Find the Bomb (see page 66), but instead of finding a bomb, Superdog and his child pals have to locate where the robbers have hidden the loot. This game can be played inside or out and will be especially enjoyed by younger members of the family, as well as by those who are young at heart. One group can hide and the other can be searchers, with the roles reversed each game.

Wrap up a packet of sweets or small toys and a special meaty chew in a box or parcel paper, together with some newspapers cut up into bundles to represent wads of banknotes. Tell the children who are to hide the stash to show it to your dog, then restrain him behind a dog gate or on the lead in the home.

Get the hiders to secrete the 'stash' somewhere inside or in the garden. In the first game make sure the box or parcel is not too difficult to locate. Later, when the children are sure your dog has understood what is required of him, it is possible to be more inventive.

When the seekers and your home police dog are ready to search, release him (if you have a whistle blow it to signal the game start) and tell the children to instruct him to 'FIND THE STASH'. Put lots of emphasis on the

word 'STASH' so that he associates its sound with this particular game. If the children and dog need a hint, send them all in the correct direction with the training whistle. Repeat 'FIND THE STASH', and sound the clicker as soon as your dog searches in the right place.

Tell the seekers to encourage the dog as he closes in on the prize. When he has discovered the stash, let him have the box or

parcel and see how long he takes to open it up. (If you have used string, take it away from the dog once it has been removed to prevent him accidentally swallowing it.) Give him lots of praise or clicks and tell him how good he is, as he bites into his meaty chew. The children can also take their well-earned prizes, and imagine what they would do with all that reward money!

Find the fellow

Is someone hiding in there?

Even the most lovable dogs like a game that has some tension. Provided your dog isn't naturally aggressive, this is just the search-and-find game for him.

What you need

- Children
- Dog gate or lead
- Healthy treats
- Dog toy
- Sweets or small toys for the children
- Optional extras: training whistle, clicker

What to do

If your dog is a guarding breed, this might not be the best game for him; it might also teach a hyperactive dog to bark in an antisocial way. However, if your dog is laid-back and calm, this game aims to teach him to search for someone in your home or garden.

Let the hider head off to hide in a corner of the garden or home. Hold your dog behind a dog gate or on a lead until the game is ready to commence. Give him a pat and a treat, then 'woof' in a low tone, gesturing in the direction of the hider. Say 'FIND THE FELLOW' and woof again until your dog barks back, just once, to make it fun. At this point release your dog.

If your dog is not the best at searching, the hider can shout out to offer a clue. When your police dog locates the hider, he should be rewarded with lots of praise and the clicker, if using. The hider should also give the dog a toy and some treats, so he understands that this person is not dangerous. Believe it or not, dogs understand the difference between training, play and the real thing. To celebrate, the children can be given some sweets or a small toy as a prize.

The ring
A magic-circle game

This game is brilliant for an energetic dog. When there is a lull in the day, bring out the ring and watch everyone have a good time.

What you need
- Hard rubber-ring dog toy
- Length of soft rope, washing line or an extended skipping rope
- Children of a similar height
- Healthy treats
- Sweets or small toys
- Optional extras: training whistle, clicker

What to do
Thread the ring on to the line and let the children hold up the line, spacing themselves about 2 metres (6½ feet) apart. When one child holds the line higher, the ring will slide away down the line. In this way they should be able to send the ring back and forth. Let them practise this first.

When playing with a dog, the line should be held no higher than twice the height of the dog – or about his full height when he is standing on his back legs. To do this, the children can either stand or kneel, depending on the dog's size. They should not lift the ring so high that the dog can not reach it.

Release your dog to chase the ring as the children send it backwards and forwards along the line. When the dog catches the ring, they must drop the rope and offer him a treat. If the ring touches a child, he is out and someone else takes his place. The children who stay in the game longest get some sweets or a small toy as a prize.

Ringing the changes
If you run a longer rope in two parallel lengths, the rubber ring can be moved down one side and then up the other.

You could also invent a points system, with points for the dog if he touches or grabs the ring or the ring hits someone. If the line touches the ground, the penalty is that the dog gets to play with the ring at once.

Spook

Catch the ghost dog

If you run out of ideas during the school holidays, you could simply switch on the TV and leave the children to it. Alternatively, try this game: it's much more stimulating and all it needs is a little imagination and a calm, friendly dog.

What you need

- Children
- Old white sheet or pillowcase (depending on size of dog)
- Healthy treats and a strip of meat
- Sweets or small toys for the children

What to do

If it's Hallowe'en night and it's not raining, this game could be played outdoors at dusk. Otherwise, ask the children to clear their toys from the floor of a decent-sized room about an hour before their bedtime and let this ghostly game commence.

Cut down the sheet or pillowcase to fit over the body of your dog – take your inspiration from the coats worn by jousting horses in medieval times! A zigzag fringe will enhance that scary ghoul effect. If he won't mind wearing it, you can include a hood with holes for his ears, nose and eyes. Alternatively, it's easy to cut a large hole through which his head will fit.

Give your 'monster' a few treats, to let him know that he's going to be a very important ghost. Then lead him outside or into the prepared room, turning off the lights, and hold on to him.

Tell the children to come outside or into the room and get them to move around quietly without talking.

When you are ready, release your friendly ghost dog. If and when his nose touches a child, she has been *ghosted* and has to go back inside or sit down in a corner of the room. At this point, call your dog back to you and give him a treat. When all the children have been caught, turn the lights on or go

back inside. Give your monster dog his final meaty reward and the children some sweets or a small toy as a prize.

If the game is being enjoyed so much that the children and dog want to play on, the rules can be modified to become three nose touches before a child is out – but make sure that neither the children nor the dog get overwrought or exhausted.

This game can be played with all good-natured dogs.

Walk the plank

A game for pirates

Will the captain and his dog fail the test and be made to walk the plank? Can your children avoid the cannonballs and win the treasure? Try this game and find out.

What you need

- Wide wooden plank and a log
- Treasure box containing healthy dog treats, and sweets/small toys for the children
- Older children
- Soft balls
- Makeshift stockade
- Optional extras: training whistle, clicker, stopwatch, eye patches, skull-and-crossbones flag

What to do

Decide which part of your outside area will be the race track. Away from the race track, straddle a wide wooden plank over a log, to make a low, safe seesaw. Designate a nearby area as the stockade.

You are the captain and guard the treasure box containing the dog treats and the children's prize. At your command, the game begins.

The children have to run along the race track from one end to the other and back again, avoiding the nose of the captain's dog as he runs with them. They can playfully encourage him, but if his nose touches them they must go to the stockade.

They must also steer clear of your (soft) cannonballs. Any pirate who is struck by a ball must go to the stockade (the dog being struck by a ball does not count).

How fast can the children run to avoid being hit by your cannonballs or touched by the nose of your dog? If they manage to stay out of the stockade, the game stops and you – as captain – must take your dog and walk the plank with him, for the children have won. Those children who are left in play can open the

treasure box and share its contents, with the dog getting his treats and the children their prize. They can then release the captured pirates in the stockade and give each of them a sweet.

Keep play periods short and make sure that your dog does not become over-excited. It may be a good idea to avoid playing this game with young children who may become over-excited themselves and tease the dog.

Hideaway room
Give him a break

Dogs sometimes need their own special place to rest, away
from the hustle and bustle of our busy lives. If he's been
playing all those new games with the children, he probably
needs some respite!

What you need
- Dog bed
- Water and food bowls
- Radio
- Indoor crate or kennel and blanket
- Old item of clothing
- Dog toys
- Filled foraging toy or chew
- Healthy treats
- Dog gate

What to do

In their natural environment, dogs are
burrowing animals. Just like their close
relative, the fox, they dig a set to protect
themselves and their young ones. There will
be times during parties and festive periods
when it will be necessary for your dog to
have a place to rest and feel secure. This
should be somewhere that children know is
his refuge, where he should not be disturbed.

Set up the dog bed in a small spare room
or storage space. Put down water and food
bowls, and install a radio tuned to a talk
channel. In one corner, introduce an indoor
crate or kennel covered with a blanket to
create a den. Alternatively, you could use
a travel bag, or even a strong upturned
cardboard box with one side cut away for
access. Don't use the dog carrier in which
you transport your dog to the veterinary
surgery, as this may have negative
associations. Inside the den, place at least
one item of old clothing that you have worn
during a brief period of exercise. Smelling of
your particular scent, this will become a
special comfort-blanket.

Walk into the space with your dog and stand there with him. Pick up a toy and make demonstrative sounds to show that you are excited by finding it. Let him explore the space in his own time, then play one of the simple games outlined in this book. Include a foraging toy or a chew and let him see you hiding some food treats.

Lead your dog out the room and go into the garden. After a brief period, let him go back in and see if he heads off to explore his new space, searching for a treat and putting his nose inside his potential den. Do not hover over him during this early stage.

If you don't have a spare room, you can use a space under the stairs or even a large cupboard that can be temporarily cleared for a particular event such as Christmas.

The key to success with a hideaway room is not to force your dog into it when guests arrive. This approach can be frustrating for dogs because, as social animals, they want to be part of the fun. Instead, you should encourage your dog into his hideaway *before* your visitors arrive, so make sure you start using the space at least a week before you will need it, to establish it as a place of refuge. The strategic use of a dog gate is advisable, because gates do not represent the exclusion from social events that closed doors do.

thinking games

Right toy

Is this the right one?

In this game your dog learns through sound-sight association which particular toy he should bring you from his box, simply on your instruction. Your friends will be amazed!

What you need

- Doggy toy box
- Three new and distinctively different dog toys
- Healthy treats
- Optional extras: training whistle, clicker

What to do

If possible, take your dog on a walk first, to clear away any cobwebs. Then, after a brief rest, bring out a new toy box containing three new toys. Say 'RIGHT TOY' at this stage so that, in future games, he will remember the sound of these words.

The next step is to teach your dog which toys are involved. Call him and instruct him to sit and stay, then praise him or use the clicker. Take the first toy and choose a simple name by which it will always be known. If it's a ball-shaped toy, say the name 'BALL' and repeat it demonstratively several times, showing it to your dog without giving it to him.

Roll the ball away from both of you, then tell him to 'FETCH BALL'. When he does so, call him and offer him a treat for releasing the ball into your hand. Repeat this three times, then put the ball away in the box.

Then bring out a second toy. If it's a rope or tug toy, call it 'RAG' and repeat the name, showing it to your dog. Throw it and instruct him to 'FETCH RAG', giving a treat reward for releasing it to you. After three throws and retrievals, return it to the box. Repeat the same exercise for the third toy. Then put the toys away and let your dog rest for an hour.

When you are ready for the final stage, take a smelly treat and wipe it on one of the toys – the ball, for example. Lay all three toys an arm's length apart on the ground, about 2–5 metres (6½–16 feet) away.

Announce the name of the toy that you have just marked with a food smell, saying 'FETCH BALL'. Your dog should then scent the ball that you have marked. Praise him or click if he does, and make a fuss of him if he picks it up in preference to the others. If he goes for the wrong toy, say 'NO' and turn away, without offering any attention.

The next time you play this game, mark a different toy with the strong smell and ask him to retrieve that one. Once he has learned by association the name of each toy, you can ask him to bring that particular toy to you from the box. Collies are especially good at this game and some have remembered more than 30 toys, each by name-sound.

Scented cloths

Smells familiar to me!

This game is a particular favourite of the scent-tracking breeds, which enjoy following their nose, although it can easily be played with any type of dog.

What you need
- Old cotton cloth
- Marker pen
- Healthy treats
- Optional extras: training whistle, clicker

What to do

Cut some cotton cloth into handkerchief-sized squares (or larger, depending on the breed of your dog). With a marker pen, number the cloth squares from one to six (or more), so that you can identify each one. Choose one of the numbered cloth squares and wipe it thoroughly under your armpit so that it collects your scent. If your dog is especially close to one family member in particular, let him or her undertake this scenting in the early days of training.

Keep your dog somewhere where he can't see what's going on while you lay the unmarked cloth squares on the ground. Then go to your dog and let him smell the scented square. Place that cloth among the others while he is still out of sight.

Put your dog on a lead and instruct him to sit a short distance away from the place where the cloth squares have been laid out. When you are ready, send him to 'GO FIND IT' (praise or click). If and when he smells the scented square, praise him or click.

If your dog 'smells' all the cloth squares, but doesn't show any inclination to target the scented one, call him to you. Take him back to the original holding place and repeat the procedure. If he picks up the scented cloth and returns to you with it (reinforce this with the clicker), make a huge fuss and give him some treats. This will encourage him to make a selection on your instructions and will harness his powerful sense of smell.

Counting
How many was that?

Harness your dog's ability to remember basic training by teaching him to count by association. Imagine your neighbour's face when your dog knows exactly how many treats he can have!

What you need

- Healthy treats
- Optional extras: training whistle, clicker

What to do

Learning will be much easier for your dog when there is a reward to be gained. This creates a positive association in your dog's mind and enables what is known as 'instrumental-type learning'.

Place a single treat on the ground and say 'WAIT'. Announce the number 'ONE' and make your dog sit and wait (or hold him on lead). Then say 'ONE' and 'OK', release him (if necessary) and let him eat the treat. For a few days, repeat this step to ensure he associates the word and the single treat.

Next time, place two treats on the floor and announce 'TWO'. His head may turn to one side and then the other, as he tries to understand what you mean. Then, after saying 'WAIT', say 'TWO' again and 'OK', to let your dog take the two available treats.

Do this randomly over a few days and then go back to 'ONE', to check whether he looks correctly for one treat, takes it and then looks at you (if you have one, sound the clicker to confirm this action), rather than searching for another treat.

Repeat the single-treat stage for a day or two, then go back to the double-treat stage, to be sure he understands the word-sound association. Announce any new number slowly and deliberately, as your dog will hear and associate the *sound* of the word with the number of treats given, rather than understanding the word's *meaning*. Make sure he hears each number clearly, and that he connects it with the corresponding treat count. He will actually hear each number as WW-ON, TOO-OO, THREE-EE, and so on.

Go fetch!

Nice work when you can get it

You and your dog can both get lots of enjoyment from simple tasks that our canine companions love to do. Newspaper, letters, keys, slippers – you name it, he will learn to bring it to you.

What you need

- Newspaper, letters, keys, etc.
- Family member or friend
- Healthy treats
- Optional extras: training whistle, clicker

What to do

Once your dog has been taught this game, he will enjoy performing basic tasks for you – especially if there's a food treat to be earned.

Choose an item that your dog can carry, such as a rolled-up newspaper or letter, or the spare house keys. Creating a scenario makes training and learning easier for both parties, so if you're using a newspaper or letter, get your helper to play postman.

Call your dog and say 'WHAT'S THAT?' in response to the sound of the paper or letter

arriving, and offer him a treat. If you have one, sound the clicker too.

Say 'FETCH' and go with him to the front door and pick up the newspaper or letter. Put it in his mouth and walk with him to your chair. Sit down, instruct him to sit and then say 'GIVE', offering him a treat in exchange for the item (sound the clicker each time he responds correctly). In a single session this can be repeated several times, provided a brief interval is left between each game.

On another day, set up the same scenario. When the delivery has been made, say 'WHAT'S THAT?' in a bright voice. If he looks at you, say 'FETCH'. If he goes to the door, be ready with a treat. If he comes back empty-mouthed, say 'FETCH' again. You may have to go with him to the door a few times until he gets the idea.

The same sequence can be used for other household items. Some dogs love this game, while others may look on bemused.

Phone's ringing

Who's calling?

There are times when you can't hear the phone ringing, but if you play this game a few times, your dog will become your very own personal assistant and answer it for you!

What you need
- Family member or friend
- Mobile phone, microwave or cooker alarm
- Healthy treats
- Optional extras: training whistle, clicker

What to do

Playing this game could promote nuisance-barking, so avoid it if your dog is already a barker. However, if you own a calm dog, the game is a great way of teaching him how to let you know, with a single bark, whenever the phone rings. The training works through reward association. Use your mobile phone when you start teaching him. Most mobiles have a range of ring tones, enabling you to choose a distinctive one that he will recognize during training.

Ask a family member or friend who is in your home to call your mobile phone on your pre-arranged signal. When the ring tone starts, sound your training whistle (if you have one) and call your dog to you, giving him a treat. Ignore him immediately after this episode, then repeat the exercise five minutes later. This time, say 'WOOF' to him when he comes. If your dog woofs back, give him a treat.

Repeat the process, but this time don't use a whistle and see how he reacts. If he comes to you and barks when the phone rings, give him a treat and say 'GOOD BOY'.

Your dog will soon get the idea and will come to tell you that you're wanted on the phone when you're putting out the rubbish, having a shower or listening to loud music. The game can also be played to teach your dog to inform you about other household noises, such as the microwave pinging or the oven alarm going off.

Somebody at the door
Your early-warning system

Teach your dog to calmly let you know that someone is at the door. Once he's trained, you can go out to the garden or have a snooze without worrying that you'll miss the bell.

What you need
- Family member or friend
- Healthy treats
- Optional extras: training whistle, clicker

What to do

It can be valuable to teach your dog the difference between family and strangers, by asking family members and friends to always knock rather than ring the doorbell.

To teach this game, ask a family member or friend to play the role of an unexpected visitor. When the visitor knocks at the pre-arranged time, calmly ask your dog 'WHO IS IT?' Then say, 'GO SEE'.

When your dog goes to check out the door, follow him at a distance. Say 'SIT', then throw him a treat to create a positive association. Blow the whistle (if you are using one) and call him back to you. Ask for a paw and say 'WHO IS IT?', then give him another treat.

When you finally let in the visitor, ask him to instruct your dog to sit (rather than giving him a fussy greeting). The visitor should then give him another treat, to encourage calmness through reward.

Practise several scenarios so that your dog begins to get the picture. Eventually, when he hears the knock on the door, he will learn by association to come up to you and offer a paw. You can teach him to woof when it's the doorbell (a stranger calling) and to offer you a paw when it's a knock (family).

This game is perfect preparation for the Sunday afternoon when you are in the middle of a catnap and your family turn up as a surprise. Your dog will wake you to tell you they are at the door. It's giving treats as a reward that does it!

Tidy toys
A clean floor!

It can be difficult to encourage children to tidy up, so just think what a good example your dog would be if he were to clear up his toys. Fun and games for all!

What you need
- Toys, including one or two new ones
- Doggy toy box
- Healthy treats
- Optional extras: training whistle, clicker

What to do

While he's out of sight, scatter some of your dog's toys (including one or two new ones) on the floor of a room. Then place a doggy toy box near the back door and put a few old toys inside. Whistle or call your dog.

Walk with him to the room with the toys on the floor and ask him to 'FETCH'. You may have to pick up one toy, to give him the right idea. Once he has a toy in his mouth, walk to the back door with him. If he stays in the room to play, walk to the back door and call him or sound your whistle.

When he comes with the toy in his mouth, draw his attention to the toy box by holding out a treat over it. Say 'GIVE', but only offer him the treat when he drops the toy, which should fall into the box. Sound your clicker then, or give him lots of praise. Say 'TIDY TOYS', then give him another treat.

Before he can think about the dropped toy, walk back to the other toys. Sound your whistle (if using), ask him for another toy, then repeat the process. If you keep the toys in the box, the game will always be fresh and you can encourage him to keep tidying up.

Wipe your paws
No more footprints

Stopping your dog from putting muddy paw prints all over the living-room carpet isn't as difficult as it sounds. Learning how to wipe paws quickly becomes a great game!

What you need

- Dog mat (available from pet stores) or doormat
- Healthy treats
- Optional extras: training whistle, clicker

What to do

This game will teach your dog, through reward, that he should give his feet a quick wipe when he comes in from the garden or after a walk. This isn't too hard for most dogs to learn, because they often scratch the ground repeatedly after marking (scenting), and such behaviour is therefore quite natural.

Put the dog mat inside the back door, or outside if it is the all-weather type. Call your dog while he's still outside and lead him to the mat. Wipe your shoes demonstratively on it. Instruct him to stand, then hold one of his forelegs and gently draw it back and forth across the mat, saying 'CLEAN PAWS' clearly. Use plenty of praise and encouragement (or sound the clicker) and offer him some treats.

After both forelegs have been wiped, repeat the process on the back legs, saying 'CLEAN PAWS' each time. Once a few sessions have been undertaken, your dog should learn that he will be rewarded for wiping his paws before he walks inside. Once you have taught him to wipe his feet on instruction, watch your friends look on in amazement!

self-rewarding games

The cube
Work for that treat!

In this game your home-alone dog will enjoy playing by himself, without any need for human interaction. Self-reward acts as sufficient motivation.

What you need
- Dry dog food (the smellier, the better)
- Foraging cube (available from pet stores or via the Internet)

What to do

Unfortunately we often have to leave our dogs at home on their own, for reasons such as work, shopping trips or essential appointments. Most dogs are happy to lounge around the house while you are away, snoozing in a comfortable place. Some are content to watch the world go by from a window. However, if your dog loves you so much that being home alone means periods of boredom, loneliness or stress, here is a great game to keep him happy.

All dogs benefit from some form of interactivity that helps make the solitary hours fly by. A foraging cube is superlative in dog terms, being more challenging than most hollow rubber toys or simple foraging balls. You can control how easy or difficult it is for your dog to access the dry food you have placed inside by adjusting the tube section that enables the release of food.

Partially hide the cube for your scent-curious dog to find, perhaps under the corner of a rug, behind his bed or under a table. Do this while he is outside or otherwise engaged elsewhere in the house, to avoid letting him see the hiding place. You only want him to discover its delights *after* you have left home. Don't give it to him just as you are leaving the house, because it is important that the foraging cube is not immediately associated with your absence. Sometimes offer the cube to him on occasions when you remain in the home, too, but otherwise try to retain its novelty value by removing it after you have returned home.

Let me at it!

Dig out that food

In this indoor game your lonesome hound can enjoy wrestling with a hollow toy stuffed with food, in order to extract some tasty snacks without any need of help from you.

What you need

- Semi-moist, tinned or dry dog food
- One or more foraging toys
- Plastic plant pot or empty cereal box

What to do

Your dog can quickly learn how to manipulate a simple hollow toy and lick inside it to obtain food rewards. These treat-filled toys can be offered to your dog in time-out periods when you are at home, or when everyone is out and your dog is at home on his own.

Force-pack some of your dog's normal food as far into the toy as possible, until it is completely filled. Semi-moist or tinned food is easy enough to spoon inside; dry food is best moistened to create a paste that is easier to pack. As an alternative, create different food layers within the toy, using a combination of yoghurt, dry and semi-moist foods. Pack in the filling as tightly as possible so that it doesn't fall out.

When your dog is in another room or in the garden, hide the filled toy under the edge of a rug or behind his bed, for him to discover *after* you're no longer around.

Initially, hide the toy in a place that's easy for him to find. Make later games more difficult by concealing the toy under a plastic plant pot or inside a discarded cereal box. The more exciting the search, the more your dog will be longing for his special toy.

Thaw delay

A surprise in the ice

This is the canine equivalent of the moment when the ice-cream van comes calling. Depending on the weather, waiting for the thaw to occur could keep your home-alone dog occupied for some time.

What you need

- Plastic cups or yoghurt pots
- Healthy treats, lightly cooked minced meat or long strips of streaky bacon
- Non-nylon string

What to do

This game requires a little preparation, but once you have made a batch of 'rewards to thaw', they can be stored in the freezer for use at any time. Save up some plastic cups or used yoghurt pots or something similar.

Fill one-third of a cup with water, then put three or more treats (or some lightly cooked minced meat) inside and place in the freezer. Once the water has frozen, put another set of treats (or more minced meat) on top, then fill with another one-third cup of water and freeze again. Repeat until the cup is filled with frozen water and treats or minced meat.

Alternatively, drop long strips of streaky bacon (either lightly microwaved or raw) into the cup so that the ends overhang the sides. Fill the cup with water, then freeze.

Outside, string up between one and three cups, perhaps from a branch or washing line. Run string through holes pierced near the top and through the bottom of the cups. Position them so they are tilted or upside down, so the treats can fall out. They should be just high enough so that your dog cannot jump up and reach them. The ice will fall or dribble out as it melts – and your dog will have lots of fun licking it away to get at the treats.

On a hot day, this game will refresh your dog's thirst and give him something to wag his tail at furiously until the reward is finally licked into shape. Make sure that he has some shelter in the garden, if he doesn't have access to the house while you are out.

Toy time
Mission impossible with a timer

To keep a dog busy, nothing beats a high-tech foraging-toy dispenser controlled by a timer. Your dog will be happy to wait as toys packed with food treats are released one by one.

What you need

- Timer-release foraging-toy dispenser (available via the Internet)
- Semi-moist, tinned or dry dog food

What to do

If you really want to spoil your dog, you can buy him a foraging-toy dispenser that will keep his tail wagging for the whole afternoon even though you are occupied elsewhere. Described as a 'home-entertainment system for the home-alone dog', the dispenser has room for several foraging toys that are released at timed intervals.

A loud beep precedes the release of each toy to attract your dog's attention and signal that a toy packed with delicious treats is about to be expelled. Dogs quickly learn to recognize and respond to this sound as a precursor to obtaining a foraging toy.

Fill each of the hollow toys with food and, if you want the rewards to last even longer, freeze the toys until the contents are rock solid. Place the frozen toys inside the dispenser and set the timer to establish when each drop is to take place. Position the dispenser in a high place out of reach of your dog, from where the dropped toy can fall safely to the ground. Your dog will soon come to associate the beep with a chance to obtain one of his favourite food treats.

Rattle and roll

Pawing for the pellets

Different types of foraging toy can provide a bored dog with a special rolling game. He may not score, but his goal is to work out how to get those treats rattling about inside.

What you need

- Rolling foraging toy
- Dry dog food

What to do

Robust rolling toys have been developed to keep a dog amused until the family comes back. Your dog learns that by pawing the toy, or by pushing it with his nose, he can trigger the release of dry food pellets. Many different sizes and shapes of rolling toy are available.

Place some treats inside the toy and, while your dog is somewhere out of sight, hide it in the area where he is normally left when you're away from home. Choose a place that he will find fairly easily, such as under the corner of an old rug, behind a chair or behind his den (crate or bed).

As with all self-rewarding toys that your dog plays with when you are out, it is important to conceal the act of hiding the toy, because this can inadvertently signal that you are about to leave him. You should sometimes offer your dog a chance to play with his rolling toy when you are at home, so that he doesn't automatically connect its sudden appearance with being left alone in the house.

Your dog will quickly learn that the reward of rolling is a scattered trail of delicious treats to munch on.

Puzzle play
Tax his doggy brain

Puzzle toys offer a real mental challenge for dogs. They can provide brief periods of amusement or be left for your dog to enjoy when the house is empty of people.

What you need
- Puzzle toy (available via the Internet)
- Healthy treats

What to do

These new foraging toys are based on children's slot puzzles, in which squares can be slid up, down and sideways to complete a picture. In the case of dog toys, when the squares are moved, a treat is revealed underneath in one of the sunken slots.

These toys can be bought from Internet stockists. Alternatively, you can try creating your own personalized puzzle toy by drilling rows of circles in a block of non-poisonous wood (such as fruit-tree, oak or beech wood). Each hole should be deep enough to hold a food treat. You will also need a wooden frame of the same size as the base, with slots on either side of each hole to accommodate moveable wooden squares that can be slid up and down. Large, powerful dogs will benefit from being offered robust versions of this toy.

While your dog is elsewhere, distribute a few treats in the slots beneath the surface of the puzzle toy. Conceal the toy when he is not watching, as the act of hiding it will signal that you are about to leave him alone. (Occasionally offer your dog the chance to puzzle-play when you are at home, so that he doesn't solely connect it with being on his own in the house). Dogs quickly learn that by scratching the surface, the squares can be moved to reveal a treat. Once that happens, the puzzle will be soon up to scratch!

Wooden toys are not suitable for dogs that suffer from an owner-attachment condition (canine separation-related disorder) and display destructive behaviour when left alone, as they are likely to destroy them.

Tennis-ball treat
Foraging fun for smaller breeds

Some smaller dog breeds cannot seem to get their teeth around the larger plastic foraging toys and soon tire of the challenge, but you can create your own softer version using an old tennis ball.

What you need
- Old tennis ball
- Craft knife
- Healthy treats

What to do

Take a tired-looking tennis ball, make a few simple cuts and – hey presto! – hours of fun for your dog. He'll enjoy chewing on the ball as much as he did before, but now he'll have the extra reward of finding some hidden treats.

Using a craft knife, cut one or two V-shaped slits in the tennis ball. Squeeze the ball so that each cut opens up enough to slip a few treats inside. Roll the ball in front of your dog so that he can hear and smell the treats inside.

Now just watch him go wild with the ball! He will pick it up and throw it in the air like vermin, or chew at it endlessly in the knowledge that something that smells of food is in there.

Once your dog has finally had enough of chewing it and gnawed out all the hidden treats, let the ball dry out in the sunshine so that it's ready for use again. Small bits of rubber are not dangerous to your pooch if he swallows them, but you should prevent potential accidents by disposing of the ball once it begins to look too worn.

garden
sports

Soccer dribbling
Dogs having a ball

In this game, your dog will learn how to dribble a ball and, in true soccer style, might eventually score a winning goal against the opposing team.

What you need

- Robust soccer ball
- Healthy treats
- Yellow and red card
- Small soccer nets or two goal-post markers, such as boxes
- Optional extras: training whistle, clicker, a family member or friend

What to do

Doggy soccer is one of the simplest and most enjoyable games of all, but make sure you match the ball with the breed. If the ball is too small, your dog may pick it up and run off with it instead of nosing it. If it is too flimsy, he may, in the full flow of enthusiasm, try to bite and burst it. That's a game-over foul, for which he should get the red card!

Begin by teaching your dog to dribble a ball (two 'dribbles' for the price of one, if the breed is a St Bernard or Bulldog!) and also to stop, responding to your instructions.

Restrain your dog, either on the lead or by asking a helper to hold him, when you first introduce the soccer ball. Many dogs will just want to run riot and tackle, while a few may watch and learn. Show him what to do and make it fun to follow your instructions with careful use of praise and some treats, and the clicker if you have one. Your dog should soon learn that a dribble and run with the ball, followed by a short pause, is associated with obtaining a reward.

To start off, blow your whistle (if using) and slowly dribble the ball towards him and then stop. Repeat this process back and forth.

Next, put down the ball in front of him and be ready to whistle and release him. If your dog cannot get his mouth around the ball, he may try to push it with his nose or

front legs. Some dogs will allow a pass to go underneath them, then use their back legs to catch or flick the ball forward.

To encourage him to stop chasing the ball, say 'STOP'. If he responds, praise or sound the clicker, and give him a treat. If he doesn't stop chasing the ball, show him the yellow card and a delicious dog treat, but walk away from him *without* giving the food to him.

Goal!

Once your dog has learned how to dribble (which may simply require a bit of patience on your part), you can take the game one stage further by encouraging your dog to direct the ball into a soccer net (or use boxes for goal-posts). Stand in the goal mouth and, if your dog scores, offer him lots of praise and pats.

Jumps
Backyard agility trials

Some dogs just love to leap over obstacles like racehorses over fences. This game harnesses that innate athletic ability, creating an agility course in your outdoor space.

What you need

- Agility jumps (or homemade versions made from logs, boxes or buckets and garden canes or poles)
- Healthy treats
- Optional extras: training whistle, clicker, stopwatch, triangular ramps

What to do

In this game, you set up a series of jumps as an agility challenge for your dog. Your pet shop will supply adjustable jumps, or you can make your own by placing garden canes or poles across logs, boxes, upturned buckets or ramps. Make sure the cane will fall off easily if the dog hits it and don't make the jumps too high, to avoid potential injury.

If you are clever with tools you could even construct your own adjustable triangular ramps. They should be sturdy enough to take your dog's weight and at the peak the height should not exceed twice your dog's standing height. If constructed with wooden grip-strips or rubber matting on the outer sides, they will be ideal for agility games, enabling your dog to make 'up and over' runs as well as flying leaps!

Plan and lay out the course so that there is sufficient space to enable your dog to run up to each jump. For the first session, put your dog on the lead. Sound the training whistle, if you have one, to signal the start of the course and then run with your dog, guiding him around your homemade circuit and encouraging him to make each jump by saying 'JUMP'. Offer him praise and a treat, or sound the clicker, every time he makes a successful leap.

Repeat the course again, with your dog still on the lead. Then take him to the beginning of the course, remove the lead

and instruct him to sit and wait for your start signal. Sound the whistle or otherwise indicate the off, then encourage your dog to attempt the jumps on his own. You should still accompany him around the course and encourage him over each obstacle with the instruction 'JUMP'.

Your dog may eventually learn to run the course by himself, but it is always a good idea to race with him so that he experiences team cooperation and benefits from your encouragement. Keep jump sessions to 15 minutes or under in hot weather, when it is important not to let your dog overexert himself and become exhausted. On a cool day you could use a stopwatch to keep a record of his time and see if he can beat his previous best.

garden sports 119

Tunnels

For dogs that love to burrow

This game can be used in conjunction with Jumps (see page 118) to create a wonderful assault course of jumps and tunnels for agile dogs that love a challenge.

What you need

- Dog or children's play tunnels (or homemade versions made from plastic hula hoops and old sheets)
- Healthy treats
- Optional extras: training whistle, clicker, stopwatch

What to do

Create one long tunnel or a series of tunnels, either by buying dog tunnels from your pet shop or using children's play tunnels. You can also make your own tunnels to suit the size of your dog, with a series of hula hoops sewn into old sheets. Lay out the tunnels in a straight line or circle. If you are using them in combination with jumps, put one or more tunnels in between the jumps.

Use a short tunnel section to introduce your dog to the idea of this game. When he has shown enthusiasm, you can fix sections together to make a more challenging tunnel.

If you have one, sound the whistle to signal the start of the tunnelling. Say 'TUNNEL GAME', then run up to the first tunnel with your dog, guiding him inside and encouraging him to run through. Offer him praise and a treat, or sound the clicker, every time he makes it through. Give him a big hug if he comes out the other side 'smiling'. This game is adored by quick-learning Collies; terriers and other breeds that enjoy digging will also take to tunnelling.

You can challenge your dog to tunnel against the clock, using the stopwatch to see how long he takes each time. Make the game slightly different each time by varying the length and position of the tunnels, making some long, others short, and placing some close together, others far apart.

Hoops
For dogs that dance

Some dogs always have a spring in their step. You can teach your dog to step – and then jump – through a hoop and back again.

What to do

Hula-aerobics for dogs can be so much fun! You'll need several helpful friends or members of the family to form a line or circle, with each person holding a hula hoop at the height of your dog's back, creating a sequence of jumps. Use hoops of a size that matches the size of your dog.

Start by teaching your dog the simple game of stepping through a hoop to gain a click and a treat. Encourage him in the initial stages by placing the edge of the hoop close to the ground and instructing him to step through the hoop.

After each successful step through, praise your dog or use the clicker and raise the hoop slightly higher, until it is at the optimum height and your dog can jump through several in succession. Eventually, you will be able to walk with the hoop as your dog circles you and jumps through.

Don't encourage him to jump too high. Some dogs, such as Jack Russells, can leap to great heights compared to their small stature, but the risk of injury means it is always best to keep the hoop a maximum of 30–60 centimetres (1–2 feet) off the ground.

Aqua dash
The wet and wild game

With just a paddling pool, you can create a 'river' in your outdoor space and satisfy your dog's need to play in water and be mentally stimulated at the same time.

What you need

- One or more children's paddling pools
- Branches or logs
- Family member or friend
- Waterproof toy or gundog training dummy
- Healthy treats
- Old towel
- Optional extras: training whistle, clicker, stopwatch

What to do

If you own a water-friendly breed, you may already play a version of this game at every opportunity. Labradors, for example, love nothing more than jumping into rivers and pulling out branches. Try this game to focus your dog's enthusiasm on a safe retrieval toy that won't harm his dental health.

In your outdoor space, fill one or more paddling pools with water. If you are using more than one pool, space them out in a straight line. Place some obstacles, such as branches or chairs, around each pool to create a barrier, leaving a space at either end of the pool for your dog to make his approach and exit.

Ask your helper to hold your dog on the lead at the approach to the first pool. Stand at the other end of the pool and show your dog the waterproof toy or training dummy. Sound the training whistle, if you are using one, and call out 'AQUA DASH', before throwing the item into your end of the paddling pool. At this point, your helper should release the dog.

Sound the whistle again once he has jumped into the water, then call him to you to promote his recall and retrieval skills. When he arrives, instruct him to sit and offer him a treat in exchange for the toy. The

retrieval toy can then be thrown to your helper so that he can proceed to the next pool or reverse the sequence from the other end of the first pool. Use a stopwatch to see how quickly your dog can do the course.

Stand well back before any fur-shaking begins – unless it's hot and you want a shower! Dry your dog off with an old towel afterwards. As always, ensure that children playing by water are supervised by an adult.

Race

Are you faster than your dog?

This is probably not the game to play with a fleet-footed Greyhound or Irish Setter. However, a naturally lethargic Spaniel may offer a little sport for energetic members of the family.

What you need

- Garden canes or soccer training cones
- Stopwatch
- Family and friends
- Race sheet
- Healthy treats
- Sweets/small toys for the children
- Optional extras: training whistle, clicker

What to do

Start by creating a race track around your garden or back yard, using garden canes or soccer training cones as markers. The layout could be a zigzag or circular course. Time with the stopwatch how long it takes for each player to race the course, and mark down individual times on a race sheet.

With your dog on the lead or walking to heel, walk around the course with him. Then the two of you should gently trot around the course and, finally, jog around it together. During each of these stages, use plenty of encouragement, praise and treats.

You may need to begin the race with some form of staggered start, if your dog is small and slow, or if small children are playing and he is much faster than them. Put the dog off-lead in the start position (sitting) and the player (standing) in sprint mode, then blow the whistle or call to start the race. Any deviation from the course by dog or person incurs an appropriate time penalty – strategically position other family members or friends to prevent shortcuts being taken by dog or humans. Most dogs will successfully run the course off the lead, although a few may need to be taken round on a short lead. The winner gets a treat (if it's the dog) or a sweet/small toy (if it's a child).

Extra challenges

You can draw on other games in the book for ideas about jumps, tunnels, hoops or even paddling pools (see pages 118–125) to make the race even more fun. While your dog is jumping through a hoop, running along a tunnel or splashing in the pool, the human participants could perform a challenge, such as trying to spin a hula hoop around their waist 10 times without dropping it.

Find the target!
Searching in the garden

Your dog knows everyone in your family and network of close friends by sight and scent. You can encourage him to use this knowledge to search for a particular person in the garden.

What you need
- Family and friends
- Healthy treats
- Dog gate or lead
- Optional extras: training whistle, clicker, stopwatch

What to do

Start training for this game by introducing by name all the 'targets'. The players should stand in a circle. Each player should say the dog's name and then call him, with a blast of the training whistle if you have one. After instructing the dog to sit and offering him a food treat, the person should say a simplified version of his or her name. For example, Stuart would be 'STU', Benjamin would be 'BEN' and Charlotte would be 'CHARLEY'.

At the next stage, one player says 'FIND' and another player's name (for example, 'CHARLEY'), sounding the training whistle if using. Once your dog has been given the chance to go back and forth among the participants looking for and being rewarded for finding Charley, the game can begin in earnest.

Restrain your dog in the house, behind a dog gate or on the lead, while the target hides outside. When the target calls or whistles, say 'FIND' and the target's name to signal the start of the hunt.

Once your dog locates the target, she should say her abbreviated name clearly and give the dog a big hug, lots of pats and a treat. This game is perfect for sighthounds, but most gundog breeds also thrive on playing search-and-find games because these are not far removed from the tasks they were originally bred to undertake. Use a stopwatch to make the hunt more exciting.

Magic pots
Is it underneath this one?

Dogs with an excellent short-term memory should be the winners in this game. However, the real winners are your family, as they watch your dog revealing his hidden talents!

What you need
- Plastic plant pots
- Retrieval toys or balls
- Dog gate or lead
- Healthy treats
- Optional extras: training whistle, clicker

What to do

Borrow up to ten large plastic plant pots from the gardener in the family and lay them out upside down in a line in your outdoor area. Place a retrieval toy or ball under one of the pots. Meanwhile your dog should be inside the home, behind a dog gate or on the lead, and unable to see what is going on.

When you are ready, walk your dog on-lead up to the line of pots. Lift up each pot in turn, saying 'SORRY' in a sad tone when an empty pot is revealed. Be ready to say 'YES' in a bright tone when the hidden toy or ball appears. Let your dog see and even sniff the toy or ball, but do not allow him to mouth it.

Now take your dog up to the starting point of the line and instruct him to sit. If you have a whistle sound it, and release him with the instruction 'FIND'. Praise him loudly if he heads straight to the pot with the toy or ball. If he picks up the item, sound the whistle and give him lots of pats and a treat when he retrieves it and returns to you with it. As he gets better at this game, you can hide an item under more than one empty pot.

Playing for rewards

If yours is the type of dog that just checks out every pot without knowing which one contains the ball or toy, encourage his searching skills by occasionally putting a treat underneath an empty pot.

Swing ball
Watch that flying dog!

If your family already enjoy batting at swing-ball, you can modify the game to make it dog proof. Then watch out for your flying dog as he chases the ball on the line!

What you need
- Children's swing-ball game (or a homemade one made from a garden brush and some string)
- Hard rubber ball on a rope
- Family and friends
- Healthy treats
- Optional extras: training whistle, clicker, stopwatch

What to do

Nothing beats a simple energetic game to get people and dogs in the mood for some fresh air. So turn off the television and games console and send everyone outside to play doggy swing-ball.

If you already have a children's swing-ball game, modify it by removing the normal ball and replacing it with a strong rubber ball on a rope. This will be harder to hit, so players will have to put more effort into batting it around. Alternatively, use an old garden brush. If possible, choose the type with a hanging notch on top, to which some string can easily be attached. Plant the swing-ball post or the broom head firmly in the ground.

Introduce the rubber ball on a rope to your dog, allowing him to watch as the players stand a little way apart and throw it to each other. Occasionally let him catch the ball by throwing it low, and say 'SWING BALL'.

Call your dog to you and give him a treat in exchange for the toy (don't play tug-of-war, as he will want to hold on to the ball). Tie the rubber ball on a rope on to the swing-ball string. The players should then announce 'SWING BALL' and start batting the ball to each other. Encourage your dog to catch the ball, but not to hold on to it off the ground for any period.

When he has caught the ball five or ten times, offer him a treat as a prize. If he is the type of dog that finds it difficult to let go of a ball initially, give him a treat for each catch.

Keep the play session down to no more than 15 minutes, then allow your acrobatic dog a much-needed rest and his reward. You can use a stopwatch to see if he can make or break a record time for a certain number of catches. When he reaches the set number, say 'GAME OVER', stop the timer and give him his well-earned prize.

Skip the dog
A game of child's play

This is a game young children often like to play in the school playground, singing 'I like coffee, I like tea, I want my friend to jump with me'. You can substitute your dog's name for *my friend*, and teach him how to skip!

What you need
- Family and friends
- Skipping rope or soft rope
- Healthy treats
- Optional extras: training whistle, clicker

What to do

The trick to this skipping game is to begin by teaching your dog to step over the rope while it is held close to or on the ground. If you have one, a clicker is ideal for the early stages of this game, especially for an overweight dog, because it considerably reduces the number of treats necessary to encourage him to jump over the rope.

One of the easiest ways to establish this game is by playing it with two rope swingers and two trainers. If adults and children are playing, it is easiest if the children swing the rope and the adults play the role of the trainers, encouraging the dog to cross the rope and helping the children take the game on to the next stage.

The four human participants should arrange themselves in a diamond pattern. The two skipping players should hold the rope lowered in the middle. The two trainers, standing opposite each other at the other points of the diamond, then call the dog between them, offering him a click and a treat each time he crosses the rope.

Encourage the dog to jump over the rope held a little way off the ground. Reward him with a treat each time he jumps it, until he gets the idea.

Eventually everyone can enjoy singing skipping rhymes, such as the one suggested above, substituting your dog's name. Make

sure you include breaks in the skipping sessions, to allow your dog to rest, and be wary of playing the game on hot days without cloud cover, particularly if there is no shade. Avoid overworking a hyperactive or very energetic dog with skipping games.

Teddy bear, teddy bear

In this variation of the game, players sing a song and then perform a simple designated task such as 'touch the ground', 'climb the stairs' or 'turn around'. You can replace 'teddy bear' with your dog's name.

Dash and splash
More paddling-pool play for dogs

This can be great fun on a hot summer's day. Set up the paddling pool in the garden, start a relay game and watch everyone enjoy some dashing and splashing.

What you need
- Dog shampoo and an old towel
- Children's paddling pool
- Two cones or other markers
- Family and friends
- Healthy treats
- Sweets or small toys for the children
- Optional extras: training whistle, clicker, stopwatch

What to do
The first task is to bathe your dog – no one wants to share a paddling pool with a smelly dog, but it's great when he's so clean that he's ready to hit the local dog show. Use dog shampoo and luke-warm water, then dry him off with an old towel.

Fill the pool with water, then mark off a race track with cones or other markers. Establish a start/finish point and a turn-around point. Line up the players, with the dog placed last in a sitting position on the lead. The player nearest the dog is the handler and should have some treats ready.

Start the game with the whistle, if you have one. The first player races to the pool, jumps in and out, then runs to the turn-around and back through the pool again, before joining the queue behind the dog and handler. The second player then sets off. When it's the handler and dog's turn, the dog should be released and encouraged to run alongside the player to dash and splash. Once he's made the circuit, give him praise and some treats. All the players can take turns to be the dog handler.

Once your dog understands the aim of the game, he can become part of the relay team

without being held on the lead. Using the stopwatch can increase the competitive element, as records can be made and subsequently broken, and the fastest player can be awarded sweets as a prize.

If your dog is a Poodle, Labrador or Retriever, water will be a powerful magnet to him, but a Boxer may need some praise and a bit of physical encouragement to take the jump. If your dog runs around the pool rather than jumping in, that's okay; some dogs may even leap over the paddling pool. As always, ensure that children playing by water are supervised by an adult.

wacky
walks

Where is it?

Searching for a hidden toy or treat

This game is a simple way of making a walk more stimulating for your dog, by offering him a reward.

What you need

- Retrieval toy (a training dummy or rope toy) or a strong chew
- Dog gate or lead (for training)
- Healthy treats
- Optional extras: training whistle, clicker, a family member or friend

What to do

If your dog has already been taught how to play search-and-find games (see pages 24–43), this one will be easily introduced on a walk. If he hasn't, begin by showing him a retrieval toy or chew while he is behind a dog gate or on a lead in your house, then hide it in your garden. Say 'WHERE IS IT?' and release him to search for it. Make the first game as easy as possible, gradually increasing the difficulty with each session.

Then you are ready to offer him this game while you are on a walk in a rural area or at the local dog-friendly park.

Wait until your dog is ahead of you, busy sniffing at a clump of grass or a tree trunk, then sound the training whistle if you are using one and call his name. When he arrives, show him the retrieval toy or chew and tell him to 'SIT' and 'STAY'. If he is not the kind of dog to remain obediently in one place, work with a partner who puts him on the lead and holds him while you run off to hide the item. Once you have returned to the holding spot, say to your dog 'WHERE IS IT?' Then release him to search.

If you have hidden a chew, be ready to congratulate him once he has located it, and let him eat it there or carry it home to devour in true foraging style. If you have used a retrieval toy, sound the whistle again to promote his return, then offer him a treat in exchange for the toy. Put it away and repeat the session later on the walk.

Tree hiding
Will he find the target?

This is a fun variation on Where Is It? (see page 140), for when your dog is off-lead during walk times. A family member or friend becomes the target for a search-and-find mission.

What you need
- Trees
- Family member or friend
- Healthy treats
- Optional extras: training whistle, clicker

What to do

This game is for a walk through woods or along a tree-lined path where your dog is allowed off-lead. When you are ready to play, sound the whistle if you are using one, and bring your dog to your side.

If he is the obedient kind, instruct him to 'SIT' and 'STAY', while your helper hides behind a tree. Keep your dog's attention by praising him, holding his focus on you and away from the person who has gone off to hide. If your dog is likely to run straight after

whoever is hiding, hold him on a lead and offer him a treat or use the clicker in return for his attention.

When you are ready to play, sound the whistle and say 'WHERE IS SHE?' Alternatively, the person hiding can sound the whistle or call to help your dog locate her. When your dog has located the hidden person, she should give him a pat and a treat. Then call your dog back or sound the whistle and offer him a treat for returning.

There can be great value in keeping your dog focused on you during walks. Not only does it mean that you are exploring as a team, but your dog will also be stimulated through his sense of sight. Most dogs are obsessed by smells and their own 'marking agenda', so it can be a bonus to stimulate him in a *visual* way. This simple game will be lots of fun for most dog breeds and can be repeated on long walks to promote recall and obedience.

Now you see it
Increase your dog's recall abilities

A good way to keep your dog interested in your instructions during walks is to motivate him with some novel toys.

What you need

- Two new retrieval toys that fit comfortably in your pockets or bag
- Healthy treats
- Optional extras: training whistle, clicker

What to do

There are times during walks – particularly towards the end, or when other dogs are running free or children are approaching – when perfect recall behaviour from your dog is a real help. Everybody wants to have a happy and obedient dog and this game uses a simple motivating trick to promote good recall behaviour.

Put a toy in each of your pockets or carry them in your bag. During the first part of your walk, when your dog is exploring scents and making his own territorial marks, sound the whistle (if you are using one) and call his name. When he arrives, instruct him to 'SIT' and let him see one or both of the new toys. Then walk on a little further, click and offer him a treat.

When he is least expecting it, throw one of the toys and instruct him to 'FIND'. When he locates the toy and picks it up, sound the whistle or call his name and be ready to exchange a click or praise and a treat for the toy. If he is the possessive kind, show him the other toy. Most dogs will want the one you have over the one they already possess.

Once a toy has been retrieved and given up, put it back in your pocket or bag and continue walking as though it no longer exists, until it's time to repeat the process a little later on during the walk.

Most dogs will follow an owner closely in the knowledge that something wonderful is waiting for them in a pocket or bag. If your dog has any terrier in his bloodline, squeaky toys will work especially well.

The weave
Teach your dog the ins and outs

An agility challenge in which your dog has to weave his way among flexible poles is a great way to test his mobility and make his walks even more thrilling.

What you need
- Hollow plastic poles or garden canes
- Carrying bag
- Healthy treats
- Optional extras: training whistle, clicker

What to do

You can teach the principles of this game in your garden, then put them into practice on a rural walk or in a dog-friendly park, carrying the canes or poles with you in a bag.

In early practice sessions, stand a line of canes or poles upright in soft ground about 1 metre (3⅓ feet) apart. Put your dog on the lead, say 'WEAVE' and start by walking him on your right-hand side. Hold the lead to direct him left after the first pole, then right after the next pole in a weave pattern. Walk all the way down the line of poles with him, weaving in and out between each one. Offer lots of encouragement and give him the occasional treat, or sound the clicker, as he passes each pole.

Once you have reached the end, repeat the weaving pattern back down the line. Repeat this training several times. If you are confident about your dog's ability to walk to heel, you can repeat the process (clicking again) with him walking the weave at your heels. Occasionally offer him an encouraging treat. If he misses a cane or pole during the heel session, call him back to you, show him a treat, but hold it back and start again.

When you are confident your dog has the capacity to weave around the poles without your guidance, move them closer together.

Then start a real game with the training whistle, announce 'WEAVE' and encourage him to work the line. Once he has truly mastered the game, take the poles with you on walks and set them up wherever you feel that a session can be undertaken.

Ready, steady, go!

Teach your dog to track

If a dog could ask, this is one of the games he would love to play during a family walk. Once he's been released, just watch him go!

What you need

- Family member or friend
- Healthy chew or chunk of red meat
- Dog with a well-trained 'sit' or 'down'
- Optional extras: training whistle, clicker, stopwatch

What to do

Driving to a local walking spot or walking your dog on the lead to a favourite location is the starting point for this game. Dogs that associate a favourite walk with a ride in the car will be raring to go as soon as you arrive at your destination. The game commences at the beginning of the walk and harnesses all the pent-up energy that has been growing throughout the journey.

Instead of allowing the family to spill out of the vehicle with the dog to start the walk together, restrain your dog, either by verbal command or by controlling him on the lead from inside the car, with a door or the hatchback open. Choose a volunteer who is naturally full of energy to act as the target. Give him a healthy chew or chunk of red meat to carry and ask him to show it to the dog and then jog a short distance away, stopping when he is still visible.

When the target is ready and waiting, say 'READY, STEADY, GO!', sound the training whistle if you are using one and release your dog with a second 'GO'. Meanwhile, the rest of the family can follow the action at a leisurely stroll.

When the dog is within 3 metres (10 feet) of the target, he should shout 'SIT' or 'DOWN' and give the dog his prize to eat while the family catches up. The clicker can be used at all stages. If you have a large or fast dog, take care that he doesn't bump into or otherwise frighten small children in his urge to reach the target.

Start with short distances when you are teaching your dog the rules of the game, gradually increasing them. If the dog seems unsure which way to go, the target can sound a training whistle for encouragement. Family members can compete against one another in the role of target, using a stopwatch to record the dog's speed.

Burning off your dog's energy in this way can be a particular blessing if you are walking a Saluki, Gazelle Hound, Borzoi or any other super-fast breed.

wacky walks   149

Jog the dog
Team keep-fit

Many dog owners like to jog with their favourite companion. You too can increase your fitness regime by jogging with your dog in a favourite park or other location where he can run off-lead.

What you need
- Healthy treats
- Optional extras: training whistle, clicker, stopwatch

What to do

Exercising together is fun, but you should avoid running with your dog on the lead as this can lead to him becoming frustrated. Bear in mind that, even if you are fit enough to run marathons, your dog may not have the same energy levels or physical abilities. Running a young dog too hard can increase hyperactivity, and putting older dogs through too tough a pace can lead to impact injuries to the joints. Regular short jogs are best.

Drive or walk your dog on-lead to your chosen location. It is not a good idea to jog with your dog off-lead through urban streets as these offer constant invitations for your dog to stop and sniff and even to try to cross a busy road to check out another animal.

When you reach the park, take your dog off-lead and ask him to 'SIT'. Offer him a treat, then start a dog-jog together at a slow pace. Praise him or sound the clicker every 10–20 metres (33–66 feet) to reward his ability to keep up with you. If he can easily keep up, occasionally slow down and then, when he least expects it, pick up speed again, to vary the pace a bit.

Keep talking to your dog the whole time as you run, giving him plenty of smiles and eye contact as well as lots of praise, in between managing your own breaths as the pace rises or slows. If you are approaching people or other dogs, show him a treat to gain his attention, then keep talking to him or sounding the clicker to keep him focused on you rather than them. Once past them, sound the clicker again, give him a verbal

congratulation and, if he's not too out of puff, a dog treat. If you want an extra challenge, you can use a stopwatch to see if you and your dog can beat your previous time over a set distance.

Keeping your dog running to heel is a good test of his obedience, but remember to keep the dog-jogs short so that you don't frustrate his natural urges to relieve himself or investigate interesting smells.

Me to you

Dash between family members

If you want a simple game to play during walks, teach your dog to dash between you and friends or members of your family, so that all his running is for fun.

What you need

- Family member or friend
- Retrieval item, such as a Frisbee or ball
- Healthy treats
- Optional extras: training whistle, clicker

What to do

This game should have its beginnings in a brief learning session or two in the garden. The first stage is to teach your dog that when a family member or friend throws a ball or Frisbee, he has to go and fetch it, but instead of taking it back to the thrower he must return it to another player.

Start by teaching your dog to run between you and your helper. Make sure that you are both armed with reward treats. You can also use a training whistle each, if you have two whistles. You should begin the game by throwing the retrieval item.

When the dog runs and collects it, the helper should sound the training whistle (if using) and encourage him to return to her. Once the dog responds, the helper should instruct him to 'SIT' (praise or use the clicker) and then say 'GIVE', in exchange for praise (or a click) and a treat when the dog gives up the item. The first step is then repeated, with you or another helper throwing the retrieval toy, and so on.

Once your dog has learned to fetch and carry an item from one person to another, the game can be played on short walks where it can be useful to encourage him to burn off excess energy. As with other very energetic games, this is not one to play out in the open on a hot day, unless it is kept down to a five-minute session. Dogs can overheat very quickly in hot weather if there is insufficient shade.

Left or right?

Teach your dog to understand direction

When you are on a familiar walk, your dog may know the route
well enough to run on ahead. To teach him about direction, use a
new walk where there are various route options.

What you need

- Training whistle
- Healthy treats
- Optional extra: clicker

What to do

A walk is a perfect opportunity for stimulating
interaction with your dog. Encouraging him to
pay attention to positive signals is not only
fun, but useful for distance control. You will
need to find a new walk, which ideally
should have lots of dividing paths and
alternate routes. As you know the route and
your dog does not, he should look to you for
direction (although in this situation some
dogs may choose to stick close to you rather
than explore). In this game your dog learns
that he can gain more off-lead freedom if he
follows your instructions.

In this game, you will use the whistle to
communicate alongside hand signals and
word sounds. Begin by reinforcing the reward
aspect of the training whistle. Sound it and
instruct your dog to 'SIT', then give a treat.
Release him from the lead and encourage
him to explore the trail you have chosen.

When the path divides, most dogs will
look for an indication of which way to go,
although some will explore the route of their
choice and then double back to join their
owner on another path. What happens next
is down to your dog.

If he looks up before deciding, give a short
burst on the whistle and hold your arm out in
whichever direction you have chosen, then say
'RIGHT' or 'LEFT'. If he chooses correctly and
you both take the designated path, reward
him with a treat.

If your dog takes the wrong path, sound
the whistle in a long burst for recall, bringing
him back to you. Then keep him close by

your side until you are both walking together on the correct path.

Working dog

The model to aspire to is the working farmer, who uses a whistle and simple signals to guide his dog to round up livestock. You can make up hand signals or use a walking stick to point out directions. Working instructions such as 'COME BY' (clockwise) and 'AWAY' (anti-clockwise), 'LIE DOWN' and 'STAND' can all also add to the fun.

games in
the park

Bring it back
Safe retrieval for dogs

Many dog breeds enjoy nothing better than chasing after a stick and bringing it back to be thrown again. This game harnesses your dog's natural talent and focuses it on safe retrieval items.

What you need

- Retrieval toy, training dummy, Frisbee or rope toy
- Training whistle
- Healthy treats
- Optional extra: clicker

What to do

If you own a dog that always picks up fallen branches in the park, asks you to throw them and then chews them to bits, this is the game for you. Chewing branches and sticks may seem a harmless pastime, but can be detrimental to the dental health of dogs.

It can be useful to start this training game in the garden, to ensure that your dog understands that returning with the retrieval items means a food treat. Dogs can be excitable in the park and asking them to concentrate is a bit like expecting a child to listen to instructions in the middle of an adventure playground. If your dog is possessive about toys, work on exchanging a retrieved item for a treat to encourage submissive behaviour.

Armed with a training whistle and some treats, begin by throwing the retrieval toy a short distance away for your dog to chase. When he picks up the item, sound the whistle and, when he comes to you, be ready to instruct him to 'SIT', then say 'GIVE', so that he allows you to take the item, initially in exchange for a treat. Repeat the procedure a few times, offering plenty of praise and occasionally a treat. If he leaves the item on the ground or drops it elsewhere, do not sound the whistle and ignore him if he comes for the treat.

When you are ready to play this game in the park, take the retrieval item with you

and wait until your off-lead dog is busy exploring his surroundings.

Give a short burst of the whistle, then throw the toy in the opposite direction or into some long grass. When he locates and picks up the item, give a long burst of the whistle. When he returns, indicate that he should sit at your side. Offer him a treat and give plenty of verbal congratulation.

Taking it further

When your dog is distracted and doing his own thing, drop the item behind you and then give a short burst on the whistle. Encourage him to search for it, sometimes pointing in the general direction to prompt him until he has located it.

Another trick is to place the item in your pocket or bag after he has given it up to you, and then walk for another five or ten minutes or until his attention has wandered. Then repeat the game, practising using the stimulus of the whistle so that you can catch his attention when you most need it — for instance, when there are other distractions in the park.

Leap those logs
Bring out the athletic hound in your dog

For some dogs hurdling is as easy as, well, falling off a log. This game introduces a little extra spice into something your dog can do quite readily.

What you need

- Branches or logs found in the park
- Healthy treats
- Optional extras: training whistle, clicker, stopwatch

What to do

Pick up some stray branches or logs in the park, then lay them out in a straight line or a circle. Small dogs should be offered single branches to hurdle; tall dogs with long legs can be given several hurdles made from larger branches. Position a dog treat after each jump.

Walk your dog on a lead around the course and let him sniff and explore, but not go over the hurdles or take any of the treats. His strong sense of smell will attract him to the food and stimulate him. With your dog still on the lead, sound the whistle (if using) and run the course with him, encouraging him to leap over all the logs. Let him pause to take the treat after each successful jump. Make some of the jumps yourself, if it is leadership qualities that your dog needs.

Always pause between races to allow your dog to rest and be wary of hot days without any cloud cover or shade. Eventually give your dog the opportunity to make the course on his own and be ready with lots of praise if he shows himself to be a top canine athlete.

You can use a stopwatch to keep a record of each run and try to improve on your dog's times.

Race me!

Dog versus human

If your dog is not too quick in the racing-genes sense, then with a little bit of improvisation you can both enjoy playing this fun race game in the park.

What you need

- Branches or rocks found in the park
- Garden canes
- Bag
- Healthy treats
- Family member or friend
- Optional extras: training whistle, clicker, stopwatch, spectators

What to do

Plan out an interesting zigzag or winding course, using branches, rocks or any other natural items in the park and some garden canes that you've brought with you in a suitable bag. Lay out the markers in parallel about 1 metre (3⅓ feet) or more apart — the track needs to be wide enough for you and your dog to run side by side. Place the canes at any strategic points, such as at sharp curves or track-backs, positioning a dog treat on top of each one.

Sound the whistle, if you are using one, say 'RACE', then accompany your dog in a stroll around the course. Initially keep him on a short lead and pause at each of the difficult parts, marked with the canes, sounding the clicker and occasionally giving him the treat; if you are not using a clicker, simply offer him a treat at various points. This will help your dog to identify with the layout and remember its quirks.

Start the first practice run, sounding the whistle if you have one. Trot around your home-made course alongside your dog, to trigger his competitive nature and give him the idea of a race. If you have been using a clicker, click without a treat to remind him of the more challenging parts of the course.

Once you are ready for the race proper, ask a helper to start the stopwatch, sounding

the whistle if using. See how fast your dog is out of the blocks as you race alongside him. Depending on his experience, you can either let him run on-lead or off-lead. Encouraging family members or friends to act as participants and spectators means that you can have a grandstand finish every time. Always pause between races to allow your dog to rest and be wary of hot days without any cloud cover or shade.

Baseball
A home run for Rover

In this game you can create your own doggy World Series in the park, encouraging your dog to field the ball and catch out the batters in return for a treat.

What you need

- Sticks or stones found in the park
- Family and friends
- Durable ball
- Healthy treats
- Baseball or softball bat
- Optional extras: training whistle, clicker

What to do

Use sticks or stones from the park to mark out four bases, in a diamond shape, for the scaled-down version of baseball known as rounders. Form two teams of at least two people, with two players to bat and two to act as bowler and fielder. Any extra players can field behind the batter to catch misses.

Before the game, encourage your dog to run after the ball and catch it when it is thrown. He should be rewarded with a treat for returning to the fielder with the ball. A whistle can be used to promote retrieval and recall, and a clicker to reduce the number of food treats.

Start with a practice game. The dog plays with the fielder. When the ball has been hit, the fielder sends the dog after it while the batter runs around the markers, trying to get back to base. Once the ball has been collected, the fielder heads for the batting base, encouraging the dog to join him.

If your dog gives the ball to the fielder, the fielder should give him a treat or use the clicker. If your dog beats the batter back to the base or catches the ball, the batter is out and the fielding team should make a fuss of him and give him a special treat. Don't worry if some of the normal rules of the game go out of the window. Just enjoy a bat and ball in the fresh air with family, friends and your favourite dog.

Go, go, go!
Challenges for dogs and humans

This game tests how quickly the canine and human players can complete a series of simple tasks. Once you've taught your dog what to do, who will win the prize for speed?

What you need

- Sticks or stones found in the park
- Healthy treats
- Basket
- Assorted dog toys
- Skipping rope, ball, quoits, dice, etc.
- Blank cards and pen
- Three containers to hold the cards, such as hats or boxes
- Family and friends
- Optional extras: training whistle, clicker, stopwatch

What to do

This game is ideal for a picnic in the park, when you've got lots of space and time. Leave sticks and stones on the ground to mark a start position and four compass points, with some dog treats at each point.

At the start position, place a basket containing dog toys such as a rag pull, tennis ball, rubber ring and so on, together with a training whistle (if using) and objects such as a skipping rope, a ball, quoits and dice.

On one set of cards write out human tasks, such as:
- Skip 10 times with the rope without tripping
- Knee the soccer ball into the air four times in a row without letting it fall on the ground
- Throw a quoits circle over an upright stick
- Throw a five or six with the dice.

On another set of cards, separately list the dog toys, such as a rag pull, tennis ball, rubber ring, etc.

On a third set of cards, write the four compass points: north, south, east and west. Then place the three sets of cards separately in the three containers.

Holding the dog on the lead, randomly pull out a card from each container: one for a player, one for the

dog and finally a compass card. Tell the first player her task and compass point. For your start signal, say 'GO, GO, GO!'. The player runs to the basket and grabs the designated item. She then runs to the allotted compass point and fulfils the set task, such as skipping with the rope 10 times without tripping. She then returns the item to the basket, blows the whistle if one is being used, and calls the dog, who is let off the lead.

The dog is encouraged to run to the player by the basket and is given his designated toy.

He has to carry the toy as he runs with the player to the allotted compass point to obtain his treat. Then the player returns the doggy item to the basket and brings the dog back to the start, ready for the next person to go.

Race against time

Timing the game against a stopwatch adds an extra element to this challenge. The game could also be limited to three tasks per team, and the fun will be which of the sides can achieve the challenge in the fastest time.

breed-specific games

Reeling in
Chase and capture

A cowboy and his faithful hound are the best of pals. Use a rope lasso and tasty morsels to make life exciting for those dogs that love to chase every leaf in the wind.

What you need

- Strips of meat or chew sticks
- Soft rope
- Bag or backpack (if game is played on a walk)
- Optional extras: training whistle, clicker, leather or gardening gloves

What to do

This is a super game for sight-hounds such as Greyhounds and Whippets, together with any dogs that have a chasing personality. It can be especially positive for dogs that display a tendency to run off at the first sign of movement during walks, stimulating them in the same way, but with an element of owner control. You'll have to be fit to run sufficiently fast to allow your dog to give chase.

Attach a strip of meat or a chew stick to one end of the soft rope. If you are taking your dog for a walk, coil the rope and conceal it in a bag or backpack. Call or whistle to your dog and show him the tasty reward that awaits him, attached to the end of the rope. (If it's a walk, do this early on.) Wear gloves if you wish to protect your hands from potential friction from the rope.

Throw your dog a token morsel in the opposite direction from where you intend to start the game and allow him to run and find it. Wait while he devours it. Call him from a distance, letting the meaty end of rope dangle down on the ground. Start to run away, encouraging him to give chase.

Just as he is about to catch up, throw the rope lasso-style as far away from you as you can. Once your dog has caught up with the tantalizing treat, reel it towards you as fast as possible. When he has the meaty morsel in his mouth, congratulate him on his success.

Search and retrieve
Training toys for gundogs

A training dumbbell or dummy is perfect for exercising the natural retrieval skills of working dogs such as Spaniels, Labrador Retrievers, Setters and Pointers.

What you need
- Training dumbbell or dummy, correctly sized for your breed of dog
- Healthy treats
- Optional extras: training whistle, clicker

What to do

Most gundogs are hard-wired to retrieve. This is particularly true of dogs bred directly from working stock. Games played with a training dumbbell or dummy reduce the frustration that these dogs may feel when their strong desire to search, retrieve and deliver is not given an outlet. These retrieval games can be rewarding for both you and your dog.

First, undertake practice sessions in your garden to make sure your dog understands what is required of him. Introduce the dumbbell or dummy and instruct your dog to 'SIT'. Let him hold it in his mouth and ask him to 'GIVE'. When he does, use the clicker immediately or praise him, before offering him a treat. Repeat this several times.

When you are ready, throw the dumbell or dummy a short distance away and say 'FIND'. Call your dog to you when he picks it up and say 'DELIVER', sounding the whistle if you are using one. When he comes, instruct him to 'SIT' at your side and say 'GIVE', clicking or praising and treating as soon as he does. Some dogs have a low attention span for retrieval, while others feel punished when the toy is not immediately thrown again, because they enjoy it so much; the clicker technique on delivery will help prevent possessiveness over the toy. Avoid reaching out for the dumbbell or dummy, encouraging him to deliver actively into your hand.

Once you are confident that your dog understands exactly what is required of him, you can take the toy on walks. The simplest

game is to throw the dumbbell or dummy for him to find, retrieve and deliver.

Training tips

If your dog dodges the delivery and drops away or dances around you, start the game with your back against a wall or fence.

If he tries to tease you from a distance with the toy in his mouth, walk away. Even if you have to walk a considerable distance, by doing so you are showing him a strong leadership stance. Once he knows what is required of him, he (and you) will enjoy honing his natural skills.

A training dumbbell or dummy can also be hidden to encourage his searching skills. Waterproof dummies can be used in wetlands or water for dogs that enjoy a swim.

Catapult ball
Launching dog missiles

This game is perfect for those swift, long-legged breeds that need to expel pent-up energy. With this up your sleeve, you will look forward to the next dog walk with real enthusiasm.

What you need
- Catapult
- Ball-shaped retrieval toys
- Healthy treats
- Optional extras: training whistle, clicker

What to do

This game suits Salukis, Gazelle Hounds and Borzois, but is also ideal for many Collies, Retrievers and Spaniels. These dogs enjoy chasing after a ball, but it is all too easy for you to end up with arm strain, as you try to offer your striding hound a decent distance to run. Instead, buy a catapult (available from sports shops) – or even construct your own while recalling your childhood days.

Once you have the appropriate launcher, you need two new toys to use as retrievable missiles. These might simply be hard rubber balls or one of the many launchable dog toys available in pet stores or via the Internet.

Lightly rub the toys with a treat to make them smell good. Then show your dog his new playthings. Launch one into the air with the catapult – not too far away for the first game. Once your dog has located the toy and picked it up, blow the whistle and sound the clicker, if you are using them, or encourage him with praise to release the toy into your hand. Put the toy away.

Send the second toy further away and, on its retrieval and release, give a treat in return for it. This will increase your dog's appetite for the run and retrieval. Catapult each toy two or three times, before saying 'GAME OVER' and continuing the walk. It is easy to overexercise a long-legged dog or to test a non-retrieval breed's attention span. Retain the catapult's novelty by limiting your dog's exposure to it.

Hidden treasure

For dogs that adore digging

Dogs are burrowing animals and terrier breeds in particular
get very excited by the chance to dig into soft earth or sand,
exercising their instinct to create a hole deep enough to lie in.

What you need

- Uncooked bone or hide chew

- Large outer cabbage leaves

- Dog gate or lead

- Optional: training whistle, clicker, digging
  implement

What to do

Your dog has tough, sharp claws and may be
raring to go with them. You might already
have noticed him putting them to use around
the home, scratching under the settee for
that favourite toy or digging huge holes in
your flower beds. This game can be played
in the garden or on walks and will harness
your dog's natural need to dig. Terriers are
notorious for enjoying *Great Escape*-type
digging sessions, but all dogs have an innate

desire to do the same. However, other breeds
may not have the same drive to demand
digging opportunities.

First, show your dog an uncooked bone
or hide chew, then wrap his reward in some
large cabbage leaves. Detain your dog at the
back door behind a dog gate or on a lead.
Let him watch what you are doing while you
bury the 'treasure' in sand or soft earth, using
a spade if necessary. Release your dog to dig,
then sit back and watch.

This game can easily be established as
part of your dog's general exercise, if you
have sandy terrain or soft earth near by. If
you do, signs of burrowing by dogs and wild
animals will probably already be visible. It is
also easy to create a sandpit or sand-zone in
your garden specifically for this purpose. As a
precaution against disease, cover the sandpit
or sand-zone when not in use, to prevent
your dog or other creatures (including wild
birds) using it for foraging or toilet purposes.

Whistle and find

Watch your dog listen and search

A training whistle is ideal for the intelligent, herding breeds, such as Collies, German Shepherd dogs and Corgis.

What you need

- Training whistle
- Chew sticks or pieces of meat
- Healthy treats
- Optional extras: clicker, family member or friend

What to do

Herding breeds love to respond to sound signals and will enjoy working with a training whistle. Establish the game in your garden, which as part of your dog's territory is where your teaching can be most productive. The game can then be played on walks and trips.

Instruct your dog to 'SIT' and 'STAY' (if using a clicker, click for correct responses). If basic training has not yet been undertaken, ask a helper to keep him on-lead in a sit. Give a short blast on the whistle and throw a chew stick or piece of meat on the ground about 1 metre (3⅓ feet) away from where you are standing. Say 'FIND' or, if the dog is on the lead, ask your helper to release him.

Point, using your left or right arm, in the general direction where the food item has been thrown, then give a short blast on the whistle when he goes in the right direction.

When he has found the item, sound the whistle twice and call him to you. Click and treat when he returns to your side. Ask your helper to call him (click and treat again when he obeys), or take him back to the starting point and instruct him to 'SIT' and 'STAY' (clicking both actions).

Repeat the process three or four times before bringing the session to a close. Once your dog has mastered your instructions, you can play the game on a walk. When your dog is exploring, throw the chew stick or piece of meat and sound the whistle once. As he searches, use short bursts of the whistle and arm signals to guide him.

Rabbit parcel

Can your dog find the bunny?

The lanky, striding breeds such as the Irish Wolf Hound, Lurcher and Collie-Greyhound crossbreeds enjoy nothing better than chasing after hares and rabbits. This energy can be channelled into a great game.

What you need

- Some lightly cooked meat
- Plate-sized pieces of natural animal skin (chamois, lamb's wool) and non-nylon string
- Length of soft rope
- Bag or rucksack
- Healthy treats
- Optional extras: training whistle, clicker

What to do

Chasing breeds have a centuries-long history of being used by hunters and poachers for their inbred desire to race after visual targets.

Prior to a walk, lightly microwave or pan-seal several pieces of meat so that they are cooked rare, then place them on the animal skins. Let your dog watch the process to stimulate his natural curiosity and anticipation. Loosely but firmly tie up the parcels with string, making sure the final bows can be pulled apart easily. Tie a length of rope to each parcel: 2–3 metres (6½–10 feet) plus enough to tie around your waist. Then take the parcels on your walk in a bag.

Let your dog run on a good way ahead, then tie the rope to your wrist or waist. Sound the whistle, if using, then run away from your dog, trailing a 'rabbit' behind you.

When he catches up and mouths the parcel, stop and say 'LEAVE', offering him a couple of treats for his obedience. Detach the parcel and let him wrestle with it until he has found a way inside to his meaty prize. (Once the string has been removed, take it away to prevent him swallowing it.) Walk further on until he begins to explore again and then repeat the exercise.

Family by name
On first-name terms

You know each member of your family by name and there is no reason why your dog shouldn't, too. Teach him using the sound of each name, then use the training as the basis of a game.

What you need
- Healthy treats
- Family members
- Optional extras: training whistle, clickers

What to do

Herding dogs – including the Australian Shepherd and Cattle Dog, Dutch Shepherd, Border Collie, Smooth and Rough Collie (remember Lassie?) and the smaller Shetland Sheepdog – have all proved exceptional at learning by sound association, but any dog can be taught, if enough patience is shown in the early stages.

For the game to be a success, it has to unfold step by step so that your dog can process the information. If he is allowed to learn in brief sessions, he will slowly come to understand, by sound association, the names of different members of your family. If he has been introduced to clicker training (see pages 10–11), the learning process will be much faster. Early training can be undertaken in your garden, but later sessions may be carried out in open areas on walks.

Start playing the game with just one other family member. Holding a clicker each (if you are using them) and armed with treats, the human players should stand 5–10 metres (16–33 feet) apart. Put your dog in a sitting position by your side or on a lead. Say your helper's name clearly and slowly to your dog, click or give him praise and treat him (to create a positive association), then release him.

The helper should then say 'COME', repeat her name and make a slight facial gesture (not too demonstrative). When the dog starts to approach, she should click or give him praise, say 'GOOD BOY' and be ready to click

or praise again and treat when he arrives. Now the helper should say your name. You then say 'COME', repeat your name and make a slight facial gesture. Repeat this several times, phasing out the word 'COME' and reducing the instruction to just your name.

Leave at least one hour between different sessions and only undertake two sessions in any one day. Repeat the process with another family member, with you as the common denominator. Only proceed to the next stage when you are sure your dog is responding to the names alone. Now the three people whose names he has learned should stand in a triangle and see if the dog goes to the right person on hearing their names.

breed-specific games

Trot the trail

For nosey dogs

This is a great game for the natural bloodhound in your dog. Once he picks up the scent you've put down, watch him go after the treats at the end of the trail.

What you need
- Large jar or wide-necked bottle filled with diluted natural juices from a fresh cut of meat or giblets
- Strip of red meat
- Large outer cabbage leaves
- Non-nylon string
- Healthy treats
- Bag or rucksack
- Family member or friend
- Muslin cloth
- Optional extras: training whistle, clicker

What to do

Almost all dogs have a great scenting ability, but this is the perfect game for tracking breeds, including the Basset Hound, Beagle, Blood Hound, Coon Hound, Deer Hound, Fox Hound, Hamiltonstovare, Hanoverian Mountain Hound, Plott Hound and Spanish Hound. Tracking breeds with a nose for scent trails just can't help themselves on walks when they lock on to something that leaves a smell. This game will liven up your dog's strongest sense and test his tracking skills.

To prepare for this game, save a jar full of meat juices from the family cooking. Just before the walk, wrap a strip of red meat in the strong outer leaves of a cabbage and loosely tie it with string to make it into a food parcel. Grab a handful of treats and place everything in a bag or rucksack.

At the beginning of the walk, leave your dog on a lead with a family member or friend at a pre-arranged starting point. Dip the muslin cloth into the bottle and smear a hand-sized spot of meat juices on the ground at the start, and place a treat to encourage your dog's anticipation.

Repeat the process every 10 metres (33 feet) or so. Lead the trail around bushes and other natural obstacles to make it more challenging for your sniffer dog. If the route diverts from the previous direction, make sure you dip the cloth and make a mark every 1 metre (3⅓ feet), especially if the dog playing the game is not a hound. At the end of the trail put down the meat parcel in a suitable spot, ideally hidden in grass, close to a fallen branch or in a bush.

Go back to the starting point to release your dog or ask your helper to do so at a pre-arranged signal or time. Then watch him follow his nose! Once the string has been removed from the parcel, take it away from the dog to prevent him accidentally swallowing it.

Water chase

Walks with a dash of water

This is the perfect activity for water-loving breeds such as Spaniels, Labradors and Retrievers. These dogs are born with a waterproof coat and a walk is never complete without them getting their paws wet.

What you need

- Waterproof dog toy or training dummy
- Healthy treats
- Old towel
- Family member or friend
- Optional extras: training whistle, clicker

What to do

When you're going on a walk that you know will offer your dog the chance to take a swim, you can introduce a game that will help make it even more fun. All that is required is a waterproof toy or training dummy and some healthy treats, plus an old towel to dry him off with afterwards.

Wait until your dog starts practising his usual paddling technique in a stream or shallow river. Then ask a family member or friend to cross to the opposite bank, giving him a handful of treats to take with him. Sound the whistle to announce to your dog that you need his attention for a game.

Bring out the toy and throw it to your helper, asking him to call your dog. When the dog comes out of the water, the helper should throw the toy back to you and you should then call your dog or whistle to him to come for a treat. After he has chased back and forward through the water a few times, throw the toy or training dummy for your dog to play with. Towel him dry afterwards.

Index

Acknowledgements

Author acknowledgements

I would like to acknowledge the helpful input of James Leyland, my brother-in-law, and of Rachel Smith, a special client, for several games including Thaw Delay and Tennis-Ball Treat, which have worked very well for my own Jack Russell. My love to Catherine for helping me sort out my early draft pages very late one night. Finally, genuine thanks to editor Fiona Robertson and designer Sally Bond for helping make this terrific little book very handsome and to commissioning editor Trevor Davies for continuing to believe in me even when the challenge of devising the last games left me happy but exhausted.

Contact Dr David Sands on drdavidsands@aol.com or visit his website: www.problempets.co.uk

Photographic acknowledgements
Special Photography: © Octopus Publishing Group Ltd/Russell Sadur. **Other Photography: Digital Rail Road**/Page One Photography 137. **Getty Images**/Mario Tama 125. **Octopus Publishing Group Limited**/Russell Sadur 2, 8, 10, 11, 14, 30, 47, 83, 84, 85, 88, 90, 92, 94, 94, 95, 117, 121, 122, 123, 140, 147, 151, 159, 160, 183. **Shutterstock**/Chin Kit Sen 187.

Publisher acknowledgements
The publisher would like to thank all the owners and their dogs for taking part in the photoshoot: Elen Cross and Reggie, Fenella Dougall and Larry, Lara McPherson and Truffle, Joanne Mandell and Sasha, Helen St Clair and Holly, Sarah Sheldon and Sooty, Angel West and Jessie, Joy Weston and Jade, Peter Wilde and Percy. Many thanks to the models: Nula Kenzie, Anna Millar, Blythe Millar and Patrick Millar. And thanks to Amelia Hotham of www.paws4walks.com for helping us find the dogs and their owners.

Executive editor: Trevor Davies
Senior editor: Fiona Robertson
Executive art editor: Sally Bond
Designer: Annika Skoog for Cobalt ID
Production controller: Carolin Stranksy
Picture research: Ciaran O'Reilly

hamlyn | **all colour petcare**

games to play
with your dog

Dr David Sands

hamlyn

To my young grandchildren, Noah, Thomas
and Joseph – and their future dogs

An Hachette UK Company
www.hachette.co.uk

First published in Great Britain in 2009 by
Hamlyn, a division of Octopus Publishing Group Ltd
2–4 Heron Quays, London E14 4JP
www.octopusbooks.co.uk

ISBN 978-0-600-61830-0

A CIP catalogue record for this book is available from
the British Library.

Printed and bound in China

10 9 8 7 6 5 4 3 2 1

The advice in this book is provided as general
information only. It is not necessarily specific to
any individual case and is not a substitute for the
guidance and advice provided by a licensed
veterinary practitioner consulted in any particular
situation. Octopus Publishing Group accepts no
liability or responsibility for any consequences
resulting from the use of or reliance upon the
information contained herein.

No dogs or puppies were harmed in the making
of this book.

Dogs are referred to throughout this book as 'he'.
The information is equally applicable to both male
and female dogs, unless otherwise specified.

DogsTrust

Dogs Trust is the UK's largest dog welfare charity
and campaigns on dog welfare issues to ensure
a safe and happy future for all dogs. The charity
has a network of 17 centres across the UK and
cares for over 16,000 stray and abandoned dogs
each year. The charity is well known for its
slogan 'A Dog Is For Life, Not Just For Christmas'
and is working towards the day when all dogs
can enjoy a happy life, free from the threat of
unnecessary destruction.

If you are interested in rehoming a dog
you can visit the Dogs Trust website at
www.dogstrust.org.uk and click on Rehoming,
or call **020 7837 0006** to find your nearest centre.

Registered charity numbers 227523 and SC037843